# Earning Earned Value

## Unlocking the Secrets of Earned Value Management

**Eddie Merla, PMP**

Copyright Page

@2025 by Eddie Merla

Published by Eddie Merla
5503 River Gable Ct
Sugar Land, Tx 77479

Earning Earned Value
A Practical Approach to Earned Value Management

First printing.
ISBN: 978-1-300-00362-5

Trademarks and Copyrights
Throughout this book, we reference and acknowledge the following trademarks and copyrights of the Project Management Institute, Inc. (PMI®):
PMBOK® Guide
Project Management Institute, Inc. (PMI®)
Project Management Professional (PMP®)

## Contents

# Preface

I have been teaching formal project management to professional project managers for over 20 years. Most of my instruction has been influenced by the Project Management Institute (PMI®), its standard publications, and various subject matter experts in multiple industries.

I teach earned value management (EVM) to students beginning their project management education journeys as well as to professional project managers studying for their Project Management Professional (PMP®) certification.

My inspiration for this book is to provide project managers with a practical guide to Earned Value Management for projects. You may find this book especially useful if you are a new project manager or an experienced project manager with a lack of formal project management knowledge.

As a PMO director (when I was a PMO Director), I prefer the use of Earned Value Management to determine project performance for the following reasons:

- EVM provides a standard simplified approach to measuring and reporting project performance. A simple summary report can determine if a project is on time and within budget.

- EVM provides an early warning system for project managers, allowing them to perform a root cause analysis and take corrective or preventive actions, when needed.
- EVM integrates scope, schedule, and cost. Variances reported through this process indicate positive or negative progress with any or all of the three primary project constraints.
- EVM enforces solid management practices. Not only does the system require solid planning but it also requires rigorous attention to capturing and reporting actual data, measuring performance, and taking corrective action consistent with generally accepted project management practices.
- EVM provides objective versus subjective analysis of project performance and helps keep the project managers accountable for project results.

The key objectives of this book are:

1. Introduce project managers to the concepts and principles of earned value management.
2. Introduce project managers to the key planning processes and practices which are required for EVM.
3. Equip project managers with the knowledge required to implement EVM for their projects.

4. Raise the awareness of the value of EVM for transparent and objective reporting on project performance.
5. Provide project managers with the structure to educate their team members and stakeholders on project performance.

Implementing and using EVM does not have to be confusing or complicated. With the aid of a few processes and a little bit of discipline, project managers can lead all of their projects to successful performance by incorporating the knowledge shared in this book.

Let's start unlocking the secrets of earned value management!

Thanks!

Eddie Merla, PMI-ACP, PMP

# Chapter 1

# An Introduction to EVM

This chapter offers a brief overview of earned value management, its background, and the benefits of EVM systems.

Effective project management requires a solid understanding of the processes for initiating, planning, executing, monitoring and controlling, and closing projects. Earned value management is an important tool for controlling projects.

Let us first discuss the importance of controlling projects. You may have invested a great deal of time, energy and effort into building a project plan for a project. Your project scope is clear with defined deliverables and outcomes. Your schedule and your budget effectively outline your approach to the project. You begin executing your project, delivering against the expectations of your stakeholders. But how do you measure progress? How do you know if you are delivering as expected against your project objectives? Is the project on track or not? If not, how do you forecast the final outcomes against your plans? This is what controlling projects is about.

The process of controlling projects should not be subjective but, in many organizations, controlling is not objective. For example, a project manager not trained on effective control processes, may inaccurately report that the project is within budget because "only fifty percent of the budget has been spent." Ineffective project control may also lead to the invalid assumption that costs are being controlled because the schedule is on track. Additionally, without a robust control process, forecasting can become very subjective.

Earned Value Management (EVM) is a tool that can be used to provide a more stringent and objective assessment of project performance. As stated in "The Standard for Earned Value Management" published by the Project Management Institute: "Earned Value Management is one of the most effective performance measurement and feedback tools for the project management discipline. The earned value (EV) concept relates budget, actual cost, and actual work progress in one integrated system that provides a reliable projection of project performance."

Earned Value Management was introduced in the nineteen sixties by the United Sates Department of Defense. As noted in a Harvard Business Review article ("What's Your Project's Real Price Tag?"): "A recent study conducted by David Christensen and David Rees at Southern Utah University of fifty-two  Department of Defense contracts validates EVM's precision in tracking cost performance as projects proceed. Perhaps more important, the work also confirms that EVM can be used to accurately predict the final cost of projects—years before completion."

The Department of Defense introduced the standard known as the "Electronic Industries Alliance (EIA)-Seven Forty-Eight, Standard for Earned Value Management Systems." This standard has influenced the development of the earned value management approach promoted by the Project

Management Institute. The standard provides thirty-two guidelines organized into the following five groups:

**Group one** provides guidelines for organization. This group addresses the need for defining scope through the Work Breakdown Structure (or WBS). The WBS is defined as "a hierarchical decomposition of the total scope of work to be carried out by the project team." (PMBOK® 6th ed.) This group also addresses the need to define the organizations involved in the delivery of the project. Guidelines are also provided for control accounts, which are management control points integrating scope, schedule, and cost.

**Group two** provides guidelines for planning, scheduling, and budgeting. Guidelines are provided for developing a resource loaded schedule which becomes the basis for planned value. Guidelines are also provided for developing the time-phased budget for the project. Additionally, this group defines how earned value will be measured.

**Group three** provides guidelines for accounting considerations including how actual costs should be accrued for the work performed.

**Group four** provides guidelines for analysis and management reports. These guidelines address how variances should be reported, what actions should be taken when variances occur, and how to determine new estimates at completion (known as EAC).

**Group five** provides guidelines for revisions and data maintenance. The guidelines in this group address the discipline required to adapt and update the baselines based on changes to the project objectives (scope, schedule, and cost). Baseline control is mandatory for effective earned value management.

With an effective earned value management system, a project manager can more effectively perform the following:

- An assessment of the project's progress and the work completed to date.
- A comparison of actual work completed to planned work.
- An assessment of whether the project is below or above budget.
- An assessment of both schedule and cost performance.
- A projection of the project completion timeframe based on objective criteria.
- A projection of the project completion costs based on objective criteria.
- An assessment of what may be driving the project's cost and schedule variances.
- A what-if analysis to determine options going forward when the project is not meeting cost objectives.
- An objective reporting of project performance.

While EVM was originally designed for large scale projects, it can be used effectively on smaller scale projects as well. EVM helps enforce solid project management practices.

Earned value management can provide many benefits and control but EVM cannot be effective if solid project management practices are not followed. EVM will not work effectively if the appropriate investment is not made in planning the project. EVM requires planning which provides an integration of scope, schedule and costs. The scope must be clearly defined. The schedule should accurately reflect the delivery of the scope of work for the project and a time-phased budget should integrate the resource loaded schedule and costs.

**Takeaways and a Prompt List**

The key takeaways from this chapter include the following:

- Earned value management is a tool that can be used to provide a more stringent and objective assessment of project performance.
- The Department of Defense introduced a standard that has influenced the development of the earned value management approach promoted by the Project Management Institute (PMI®).
- Earned value management can provide many benefits and control but EVM cannot be effective if solid project management practices are not followed.

Consider the following prompt list of questions as you consider the implementation of EVM for your project or organization:

- Can an EVM system help your project or organization to more effectively manage project performance?
- Is your team using best practices for planning scope, schedule, and cost baselines? Does your team use baselines?

- Can you benefit as a project manager from using EVM techniques?
- Can your organization benefit from the use of standard planning and EVM practices?

# Chapter 2

## Principles of EVM

Understanding earned value management can seem intimidating at first. In this chapter, we will introduce some of the core principles and key terms of earned value management. Terms will be introduced in the description of the core principles. The following are ten core principles for earned value management:

**One:** All of the work of the project should be defined. Use the work breakdown structure (WBS) to organize the work of the project. The WBS is the decomposition of the scope identified in the project scope statement. Work should be decomposed to the lowest level of work, the work packages. The best practice promoted by the Project Management Institute, is that the WBS should reflect one hundred percent of the work to be performed by the project, nothing more and nothing less. This is sometimes called the "one hundred percent rule."

**Two:** Define the project organization. This is typically done through an organizational breakdown structure (OBS). An OBS is defined as "a hierarchical representation of the project organization, which illustrates the relationship between project activities and the organizational units that will perform those activities." (PMBOK® 6th ed.)

**Three:** Integrate the WBS and the OBS to create control accounts. Control accounts are defined as "management control points where scope, budget, actual cost, and schedule are integrated and compared to earned value for performance measurement."

**Four:** Schedule the work of the project. The schedule should include all activities of the project up to the completion of the project and should include milestones which can be used to measure progress. Milestones are defined as significant points or events in a project. Milestones can be used to indicate the planned completion of a phase or the completion of a project or product deliverable.

**Five:** Establish the Performance Measurement Baseline (PMB). The PMB is the integration of the scope, schedule and cost baselines. Once approved, this baseline can only be changed through formal change control processes. Actual performance will be measured against the PMB.

**Six:** Collect actual costs in accordance with accounting guidelines to ensure costs are associated with the budgeted work.

**Seven:** Determine cost and schedule variances and generate performance reports. The following measures are used to determine cost and schedule variances:

- Earned value (EV). Earned value is defined as "the measure of work performed expressed in terms of the budget authorized for that work." (PMBOK® 6th ed.) Different techniques can be used to calculate earned value. Those techniques would be determined prior to beginning work on the project. EV is compared against actual costs (AC) to determine a cost variance. EV is also compared against the planned value (PV) to determine a schedule variance.

- Actual cost (AC). Actual costs are defined as "the realized cost incurred for the work performed on an activity during a specific time period." (PMBOK® 6th ed.) Rules for collecting actual costs would be determined prior to starting the project work.
- Planned value (PV). Planned value is "the authorized budget assigned to scheduled work." (PMBOK® 6th ed.) Planned value at any data reporting date is the value of the work that should have been completed at that time. Total planned value for the project is equal to the baseline budget.

**Eight:** Implement corrective actions in response to significant variances.

**Nine:** Maintain estimates at completion (EAC). These estimates at completion can be determined using various methods. The EAC is compared against the original budget at completion (BAC) to determine if corrective or management actions may be required. For example, if the EAC is determined to be two hundred thousand dollars and the budget at completion is one hundred and seventy-five thousand dollars, then analysis will be required to determine if corrective actions are required or if a change may be required to increase the project performance budget.

**Ten:** Incorporate changes to the Performance Measurement Baseline (PMB) in a timely manner. Changes to scope, schedule or costs can affect the PMB. Project change management procedures are typically provided to the project management team to ensure that changes are properly authorized, tracked and recorded. Replanning and establishing new baselines may be required to support the changes.

You have been introduced to some of the core principles and key terms of earned value management. The ten principles introduced stress the importance of the discipline required for planning to set the stage for effective project controlling using earned value management.

**Takeaways and a Prompt List**

The key takeaways from this chapter include the following:

- All of the work of the project should be defined. Use the work breakdown structure (WBS) to organize the work of the project.
- Establish the Performance Measurement Baseline (PMB). The PMB is the integration of the scope, schedule and cost baselines.
- Determine cost and schedule variances and generate performance reports.

Consider the following prompt list of questions as you consider the implementation of EVM for your project or organization:

- Do you understand the ten core principles for EVM and how well is your project or organization aligned with these principles?
- What areas of project management require improvement to accommodate EVM?
- Does your organization support EVM practices and standards or do they need to be developed?

# Chapter 3

# EVM and the Project Life Cycle

Earned value management is a structured approach which begins before the project even begins. In this chapter, we will explore the stages of EVM by identifying activities which influence EVM in the project management process groups defined by the Project Management Institute: Initiating, Planning, Executing, Monitoring and Controlling and Closing.

## Initiating

In initiating, the project charter is developed and stakeholders are identified. The project charter begins the scoping of the project and identifies constraints and assumptions which may influence the EVM process.

Additionally, EVM may be considered an organizational process asset (OPA). Organizational process assets are defined as "plans, processes, policies, procedures, and knowledge bases specific to and used by the performing organization." The project should use the organizational guidelines for EVM, if there any.

The project management office (PMO), if one exists, can provide expertise and guidance in using EVM for the project. Decisions regarding the tailoring of the EVM processes should be identified in the project charter.

The project charter should also indicate whether EVM methods are required for the project. In certain situations, use of an EVM may be mandated by contract. The project charter may also identify significant risks which might drive the need for EVM methods on the project.

Knowing and understanding the stakeholders' needs is also relevant to EVM. Certain stakeholders may require EVM performance reports.

## Planning

In planning, the following essential activities set the stage for EVM:

- The scope management plan is developed. This plan provides direction to the team on all scope related activities.
- The project scope is detailed.
- The work breakdown structure (WBS) and the WBS dictionary are developed.
- The scope baseline which is comprised of the project scope statement, the WBS, and the WBS dictionary is finalized and becomes the foundation for the project performance baseline.
- The resource loaded project schedule is developed and baselined.
- The cost management plan is developed. The cost management plan provides direction to the team regarding all cost related activities including EVM.
- A time-phased budget is developed.
- Planning processes for Quality, Resources, Communications, Risk, Procurement, and

Stakeholder Engagement are completed. While all of these areas may influence EVM, resources and risk may directly impact the development of the project measurement baseline (PMB).

- In resource management, an organizational breakdown structure (OBS) and a resource assignment matrix are developed.
- The three baselines (scope, schedule, and cost) are integrated to form the performance measurement baseline (PMB).
- Control accounts are established. Control accounts are defined as "management control points where scope, budget, actual cost, and schedule are integrated and used for comparison to actual earned value for performance measurement." (PMBOK® 6th ed.)
- Contingency and management reserves are also determined.

## Executing

In executing, data collection processes are used to collect data relevant to performance. The work performance data can include data relevant to scope completion, schedule progress, resource usage, and actual costs.

The following are types of work performance data collected and reported through the execution processes:

- Percentage of work completed against planned scope.
- Actual start and finish dates for project activities.

- Schedule progress (such as milestones achieved and activities completed).
- Actual costs incurred (or accrued).
- Actual resource hours worked.
- Material consumption and inventory usage
- Procurement status and contract performance updates.
- Issues and changes identified during execution.
- Risk updates (realized risks, dropped or changed, risks, new risks).
- Change requests initiated.
- Earned value.

Project changes may be initiated during project execution for any number of reasons:

- Unforeseen risks that have materialized, requiring adjustments to scope, schedule, or resources.
- Discovery of errors, omissions, or ambiguities in project documentation or deliverables.
- Requests from the team or stakeholders to alter project objectives, features, or deliverables.
- External factors such as regulatory changes, market shifts, or new compliance requirements.
- Technological advancements or new tools that offer opportunities for improvement.
- Resource availability issues, including personnel, materials, or equipment constraints.
- Integration issues with other projects or organizational initiatives.

- Lessons learned from earlier project phases that suggest beneficial modifications.

Project changes initiated during executing need to be approved through the change control processes. Once approved, they are integrated into the work and the planning documents are updated to reflect the changes.

**Monitoring and Controlling**

In monitoring and controlling, actual costs, schedule and scope are compared against the performance measurement baseline (PMB) for the purpose of determining project performance and producing work performance reports.

Examples of work performance reports include:

- Performance dashboards summarizing progress against key metrics.
- Earned Value Management (EVM) reports detailing cost and schedule variances.
- Trend analyses tracking changes over time in project indicators.
- Status reports providing current state of deliverables and milestones.
- Risk and issue logs with updates on mitigation actions.
- Change request summaries and impact analyses.
- Resource utilization reports (planned versus actual).
- Quality reports outlining inspection and test results.
- Vendor performance reports.

Forecasts for cost and schedule to completion are determined and corrective actions are taken.

Change requests may be initiated to modify the performance baselines. These changes need to be approved through the change control processes. Once approved, they are integrated into the work and the planning documents are updated to reflect the changes.

PMBOK® Data Flow

The diagram in Exhibit 3.1 illustrates the flow of data through the processes as defined by the PMBOK®.

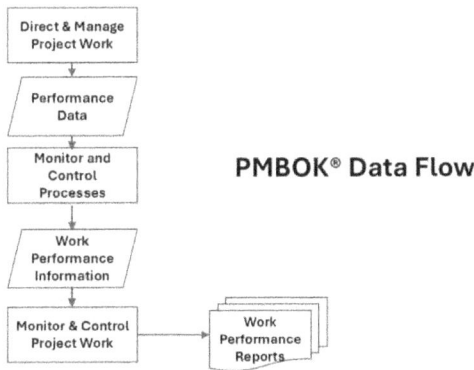

```
┌─────────────────┐
│ Direct & Manage │
│  Project Work   │
└─────────────────┘
         ↓
   ╱────────────╱
  ╱ Performance ╱
 ╱     Data    ╱
╱────────────╱
         ↓
┌─────────────────┐
│   Monitor and   │        PMBOK® Data Flow
│    Control      │
│   Processes     │
└─────────────────┘
         ↓
   ╱────────────╱
  ╱    Work     ╱
 ╱ Performance ╱
╱ Information ╱
         ↓
┌─────────────────┐      ┌─────────────────┐
│Monitor & Control│─────→│      Work       │
│  Project Work   │      │  Performance    │
└─────────────────┘      │    Reports      │
                         └─────────────────┘
```

Exhibit 3.1: Data Flow Diagram

The "direct and manage project work" process collects and reports work performance data or the "raw" data. This data is then used as input to the monitoring and controlling processes (such as control scope, control schedule, and control costs). The monitor and control processes perform the comparisons to the plan and produce work performance information. The "monitor and control project work" process summarizes the work performance information and produces the work performance reports. These reports are then distributed as determined by communications management plan.

## Closing

In closing, the project performance will be summarized along with an accounting of any changes to the baselines throughout the project timeframe.

Lessons learned regarding EVM and project performance reporting will be used to update the organization's lessons learned repository and knowledge bases. Continuous improvement opportunities are recorded.

## Takeaways and a Prompt List

The key takeaways from this chapter include the following:

- The project charter begins the scoping of the project and identifies constraints and assumptions which may influence the EVM process.
- The scope, schedule, and cost baselines are created during planning.
- During project execution, work performance data is collected, project changes may be initiated, and approved changes are implemented.
- During monitoring and controlling, actual costs, schedule and scope are compared against the baselines to determine project performance. Work performance reports are produced.

- In closing, the project performance will be summarized along with an accounting of any changes to the baselines.

Consider the following prompt list of questions as you consider the implementation of EVM for your project or organization:

- Does your PMO, if you have one, provide processes and procedures for EVM?
- Is project performance reporting discussed during initiation of the individual projects? Is EVM considered during project initiation?
- Does project planning for your projects include planning for EVM?
- Do your projects allow for the capture of work performance data during executing?
- Do your projects produce work performance reports to include EVM reporting?
- Do your projects include processes for collecting and reporting lessons learned, specifically for performance reporting?

# Chapter 4

# Organizational Support for EVM

In this chapter, we will explore organizational support for EVM.

What does it take for earned value management to be successfully applied in an organization? It takes more than just a willingness to apply earned value by project managers. The organization can provide support to ensure that project managers can successfully implement EVM processes and reporting.

For the implementation of earned value management to be successful in an organization, the following factors should be considered:

**Senior management support.** Support for the setup and application of earned value management occurs through the funding and authorization of resources for organizational assets needed for earned value management.

Management support is required for establishing and resourcing a project management office (PMO) which establishes policies, standards, processes, procedures, and governance for EVM practices.

Management support may be necessary to overcome objections to the discipline required for EVM.

Proper management support can influence stakeholders to understand that EVM is a necessary investment for project success.

**Project Management Office (PMO).** A well-structured Project Management Office (PMO) is pivotal for the successful deployment and sustainability of earned value management (EVM) within an organization. The PMO acts as a central hub, developing and promoting standardized policies, procedures, templates, and tools essential for integrating EVM into everyday project practices. By establishing clear governance and oversight mechanisms, the PMO ensures uniformity and compliance in how EVM is executed across projects.

The PMO also plays a key role in providing training and guidance to project managers and teams, building organizational competency in EVM concepts, tools, and reporting. Through targeted education and mentoring, the PMO demystifies EVM, addressing concerns and resistance related to its perceived complexity or discipline demands.

Additionally, the PMO facilitates the selection and integration of technology solutions that support EVM, such as project management information systems or scheduling software. It also maintains repositories for lessons learned, performance data, and historical project metrics, allowing teams to leverage organizational process assets for more accurate planning and forecasting.

The PMO also serves as a bridge between project teams and senior management, communicating the value of EVM and advocating for necessary resources.

**Organizational process assets.** Earned value management processes and procedures are essential process assets for an organization. Additional process assets that aid in the EVM process include but are not limited to estimating standards, planning standards, change management processes, and systems, accounting procedures, costing processes, historical information, knowledge transfer assets, lessons learned, and governance processes.

Additionally, lessons learned from previous projects and archived performance reports can be useful organizational process assets when planning a project.

**Environmental factors.** Factors that influence the setup and application of earned value management include but are not limited to organizational culture, supportive environment, risk tolerance, resource availability for the application of EVM, project management maturity, and governance at the portfolio, program, and project levels.

Other environmental factors worth considering include:

- Regulatory and contractual requirements for cost control and project reporting. These requirements may dictate not only the use of EVM, but also the level of detail, reporting frequency, and data integrity standards. Early identification and integration of these external mandates are essential to prevent non-compliance and potential rework.
- The organization's technology infrastructure may impact the ease and effectiveness of EVM. Consider whether existing project management information systems, scheduling tools, and financial databases are compatible with EVM processes. Gaps in

technology may require investment in new software, integration efforts, or system upgrades.

- The degree of buy-in from key stakeholders including clients, sponsors, team members, and even external partners can make or break EVM adoption. Assess whether stakeholders are informed, supportive, and have realistic expectations about the discipline and transparency EVM introduces. Resistance or misunderstanding may require mitigation through communication, change management, or targeted training.
- Introducing EVM often requires changes to established processes and behaviors. Gauge the organization's general capacity for change. Are there mechanisms in place for facilitating, tracking, and supporting process transitions? Organizations with a track record of successful change initiatives are better positioned to implement EVM smoothly.
- Reliable EVM depends on accurate, timely, and complete data. Evaluate the maturity and reliability of your data sources such as cost tracking, labor reporting, and schedule updates. Poor data quality can undermine the value of EVM by generating misleading performance metrics.
- External factors, such as inflation, labor market fluctuations, or supply chain disruptions, can significantly affect project costs and schedules. Awareness of these external factors enables proactive risk identification and more robust contingency planning within EVM frameworks.

- For organizations operating in multiple locations or across borders, consider the impact of geographic dispersion and cultural diversity. Variations in local practices, languages, time zones, and regulatory environments may require tailored approaches to EVM implementation, training, and communication.

A solid understanding of environmental factors ensures that the adoption of EVM is not only technically sound but also aligned with the environment in which the organization and its projects operate. By anticipating and planning for these additional considerations, project leaders can foster a more resilient, adaptable, and ultimately successful earned value management environment.

**Training and knowledge transfer.** An organization committed to effective EVM should consider investing in training and knowledge transfer assets. Project managers should be trained in project management and earned value management practices. Special training may also be required for the detailed planning for a major client or government project requiring EVM.

As EVM requires a disciplined approach to planning, training programs should include training on project management fundamentals as well as detailed training in planning (scope, schedule, and cost).

**Project management staffing.** Project managers should have the appropriate knowledge and experience to manage projects requiring earned value management. They should have the discipline to ensure that the proper investment is made in the planning processes to develop the performance measurement baseline. Project schedulers and cost controllers can also be essential project resources on major projects.

While earned value management can be applied to a project without organizational standards and support, project performance reporting can be improved significantly with organizational support. A project management office (PMO) can provide the leadership and discipline to implement and support earned value management.

## Takeaways and a Prompt List

The key takeaways from this chapter include the following:

- Proper management support can influence stakeholders to understand that EVM is a necessary investment for project success.
- A well-structured Project Management Office (PMO) can ensure the successful implementation and sustainability of earned value management (EVM) within an organization.
- Earned value management processes and procedures are essential process assets for an organization.
- A solid understanding of environmental factors ensures that the adoption of EVM is not only technically sound but also aligned with the environment in which the organization and its projects operate.

Consider the following prompt list of questions as you consider the implementation of EVM for your project or organization:

- Do your organization have the appropriate management support for EVM?

- Does your PMO, if you have one, provide EVM processes, procedures, templates, and other organizational assets for EVM?
- Does your organization support project management, planning, and EVM training programs for its project managers?
- Do the project managers in your organization understand the many environmental factors which can affect the successful implementation of EVM?

# Chapter 5

# Planning for EVM

In this chapter, we will explore the planning which is essential to earned value management on a project. The planning processes which directly affect the setup and execution of earned value analysis and management include:

- Scope management planning.
- Schedule management planning.
- Cost management planning.
- Resource management planning.
- Integrated project management planning.

Let's explore these in more detail:

**Scope Management Planning**

This process is critical because scope is the foundation for earned value management. The purpose of this process is to provide the project manager and the project team with guidelines and considerations for scope management on the project. The key output of this process is the scope management plan.

The components of this plan relevant to earned value management include the following:

- Guidelines for conducting the scope processes which directly contribute to the development of the scope baseline.

- Definitions and guidelines for the work breakdown structure (WBS). The WBS decomposes the work of the project into manageable components called the work packages. The plan defines the templates to be used for the project. Additionally, guidelines for the coding of accounts would be provided. The code of accounts is defined as "a numbering system used to uniquely identify each component of the work breakdown structure." The numbering system will also be used to organize the schedule and the budget.
- Guidelines for work packages. Work packages are defined as the lowest level of the WBS for which cost and duration are estimated and managed. Although the guidelines may vary among organizations and the type of work, a general rule of thumb for the size of the work package is to keep the work between eight and eighty hours. Another rule of thumb is that the schedule completion for a work package should not exceed two time reporting periods.
- Guidelines for planning packages. Planning packages are units of work at the work package level but lack sufficient detail to accurately schedule.
- Definitions and guidelines for developing the WBS dictionary. The WBS dictionary provides detailed information for the work packages. This detailed information could include activities required to complete the work packages, schedule information, assumptions and constraints, cost estimates, acceptance criteria and any other detail information to help the team as it develops the schedule and the budget for the project.
- Guidelines for the development and maintenance of the scope baseline. The scope baseline is the approved version of the project scope statement, the WBS, and the WBS dictionary.

- Guidelines for changes to the scope baseline. These guidelines detail the required documentation and justification for proposed changes, the process for submitting and reviewing change requests, and the approvals required to approve or reject changes. The plan may also specify criteria for what constitutes a significant change that warrants baseline revision, and outline the steps for updating project documents and communicating changes to relevant stakeholders. By establishing a structured approach to scope changes, the plan helps maintain project control and ensures that all modifications are evaluated for their impact on objectives, resources, and schedule before implementation.
- Guidelines, procedures, and tools for the validation of deliverables.
- Techniques to be used to control and measure variance from the scope baseline. This would include monitoring adherence to the scope to control scope creep (unauthorized expansion of the scope).

Another key output of scope management planning is the requirements management plan. A requirements management plan is a crucial document that outlines how the project's requirements will be identified, documented, analyzed, managed, and controlled throughout the project lifecycle. Effective requirements management is fundamental to delivering a successful project, as it ensures that stakeholder needs are understood and met, changes are controlled, and project objectives remain clear and achievable.

The requirements management plan also details the procedures for managing changes to requirements, including how changes are proposed, documented, reviewed, approved, or rejected.

**Schedule Management Planning**

We will now take a look at schedule management planning. This process produces the schedule management plan. This plan provides direction to the team for developing, monitoring and controlling the schedule baseline. The components of the schedule management plan relevant to earned value management include the following:

- Guidelines for developing time estimates for the activities of the project.
- Guidelines for ensuring all project activities are included in the schedule.
- Guidelines for milestones on the project. A milestone is defined as "a significant point or event in a project." An example of a guideline in the plan for a milestone could be: "milestones should be included in the plan for the completion of every work package." If the project is conducted through a series of phases, milestones can be used to signify the completion of each phase.
- Formulas to be used to determine schedule variance on the project.
- Acceptable tolerance limits for variance to the schedule.
- Guidelines for making changes to the schedule baseline.

**Cost Management Planning**

Cost management planning produces the cost management plan. This plan will provide direction to the team for developing, monitoring, and controlling the cost baseline.

This plan will also provide specific directions for earned value management on the project. The components of the cost management plan relevant to earned value management include the following:

- Guidelines for estimating the costs of the project activities.
- Guidelines for developing the budget for the project.
- Guidelines for developing the contingency and management reserves. A contingency reserve set aside for "known unknowns" is included in the cost baseline. A contingency reserve is used to cover known risks. A management reserve is included in the overall budget but is not included in the cost baseline. The management reserve is set aside to cover unexpected work usually required due to unexpected situations or risks. Once these reserves have been determined, the contingency reserve is used by the project manager to help manage the cost baseline. The management reserve is to be used for unexpected risks and use of this reserve requires management approval.
- Guidelines for creating the cost baseline.
- Definitions of earned value and how earned value will be determined on the project.
- Guidelines for defining and managing control accounts. A control account is defined as "a management control point where scope, budget, actual cost, and schedule are integrated and compared to earned value for performance measurement."
- Procedures for capturing actual costs on the project. In some cases, depending on the cost item, actual costs may have to accrued. Accrued costs is actual costs incurred as opposed to an invoice payment.
- Formulas to be used to determine cost variances.

- Acceptable tolerance limits for variance to the cost baseline.
- Guidelines for making changes to the cost baseline.

**Resource Management Planning**

Resource management planning creates the resource management plan. This plan defines how the resources for the project will be identified, acquired, and managed. Key components of this plan relevant to earned value management include the following:

- Resource requirements for the project. These can include both human and physical (non-human) resources. Resources are aligned with the activities of the project.
- Resource calendars. Every resource on the project has a resource calendar. A resource calendar is defined as "a calendar that identifies the working days and shifts upon which each specific resource is available." The availability of resources may affect the project schedule.
- Organizational breakdown structure (OBS). An OBS is defined as "a hierarchical representation of the project organization, which illustrates the relationship between project activities and the organizational units that will perform those activities." An organizational breakdown structure will decompose the organization into departments or groups to be performing the work of the project. Exhibit 5.1 illustrates a simple example of an OBS, which visually indicates the organizations involved in the project.

Example:
Organizational Breakdown Structure (OBS)

```
                        ┌──────────────────┐
                        │   PMO Upgrade    │
                        │     Project      │
                        └──────────────────┘

┌──────────────┐  ┌──────────────┐  ┌────────────────┐  ┌──────────────────┐
│PMO Department│  │IT Department │  │Quality Dept    │  │Human Resources   │
│     1.0      │  │     2.0      │  │     3.0        │  │     4.0          │
└──────────────┘  └──────────────┘  └────────────────┘  └──────────────────┘

 Costing Group     IT Security       Project            Change Mgt
     1.1              2.1            Support               4.1
                                       3.1
 Scheduling          IT             Standards          Training &
   Group          Development         Group           Development
    1.2              2.2               3.2                 4.3
  PMO                                 Quality
 Compliance       IT Operations      Assurance
    1.3              2.3               3.3
  PMO                                Continuous
 Governance       IT Customer       Improvement
    1.4            Service              3.4
                     2.4
```

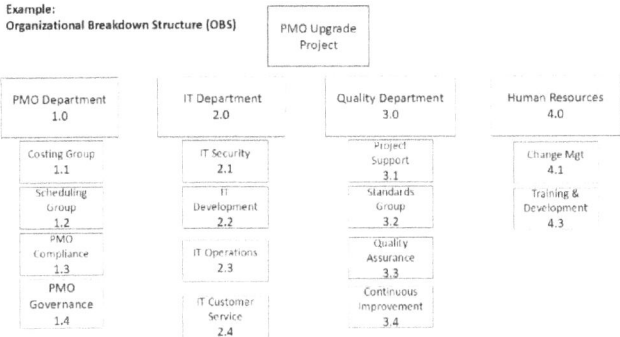

Exhibit 5.1: OBS Example

- Resource breakdown structure (RBS). An RBS is defined as "a hierarchical representation of resources by category and type." The RBS is developed from the resource requirements for the project. This tool will be used as an input to acquire the resources for the project. See exhibit 5.2 for a simple example.

**Resource Breakdown Structure**

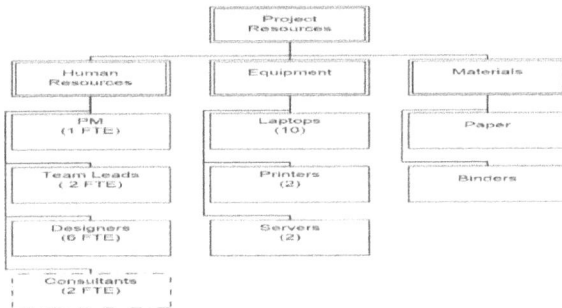

```
                    ┌──────────────┐
                    │   Project    │
                    │  Resources   │
                    └──────────────┘

  ┌──────────────┐  ┌──────────────┐  ┌──────────────┐
  │   Human      │  │  Equipment   │  │  Materials   │
  │  Resources   │  │              │  │              │
  └──────────────┘  └──────────────┘  └──────────────┘

      PM              Laptops           Paper
    (1 FTE)            (10)

   Team Leads         Printers          Binders
    (2 FTE)             (2)

   Designers          Servers
    (6 FTE)             (2)

  Consultants
   (2 FTE)
```

Exhibit 5.2: RBS Example

- Resource assignment matrix (RAM). A RAM is used to assign responsibilities of work to an organization or individual. A RACI chart is a popular type of a responsibility assignment matrix. The "R" indicates who is responsible. The "A" indicates who is accountable. The "C" indicates who will be consulted. The "I" indicates who will be informed. See exhibit 5.3 for an example of a RACI chart.

| Functions | Team Lead | John | Jane | Allen | Sue | Rob |
|---|---|---|---|---|---|---|
| - Host weekly meetings | R/A | C | C | C | C | C |
| - Collect operations data | I | R/A | C | C | C | C |
| - Produce reports | A | | R | | | |
| - Conduct daily briefings | A/R | C | C | C | C | C |
| - Monitor and control costs | A | C | C | R | C | C |

Legend:
R = Responsible; A = Accountable; C = Consult; I = Inform

Exhibit 5.3: RACI Chart

## Integrated Project Management Planning

Integrated project management planning creates the integrated project management plan, which is the integration of the project baselines and the supporting planning documents. A typical integrated project management plan may include (but is not limited to) the three primary baselines (scope, schedule, and cost) plus all the supporting management plan documents. This integrated plan serves as a blueprint for project execution and control, ensuring all aspects of the project are aligned and coordinated. Once approved, any modifications to the plan are managed through formal change control procedures to maintain project integrity and alignment with objectives.

## Takeaways and a Prompt List

The key takeaways from this chapter include the following:

- Scope management planning provides the project manager and the project team with guidelines and considerations for developing, monitoring and controlling the scope baseline on the project.
- Schedule management planning provides the project manager and the project team direction for developing, monitoring and controlling the schedule baseline.
- Cost management planning provides guidelines for developing, monitoring, and controlling the cost baseline. It also provides the team with specific directions for conducting earned value analysis on the project.
- Resource management planning defines how the resources for the project will be identified, acquired, and managed.
- Integrated project management planning creates the integrated project management plan, which is the integration of the project baselines and the supporting planning documents.

Consider the following prompt list of questions as you consider the implementation of EVM for your project or organization:

- Do your project managers create planning documents for scope, schedule, cost, and resource management?
- Does your organization support cost management planning to include the specific directions to applying EVM on their projects.

- Do your project managers develop integrated project management plans?

# Chapter 6

## Building the Performance Baseline

In this chapter, we will explore the journey of a project to the performance measurement baseline (PMB). The PMB is critical to the successful application of earned value management.

The PMB is the integration of three baselines: the scope baseline, the schedule baseline, and the cost baseline.

Exhibit 6.1 demonstrates the journey from requirements to the PMB.

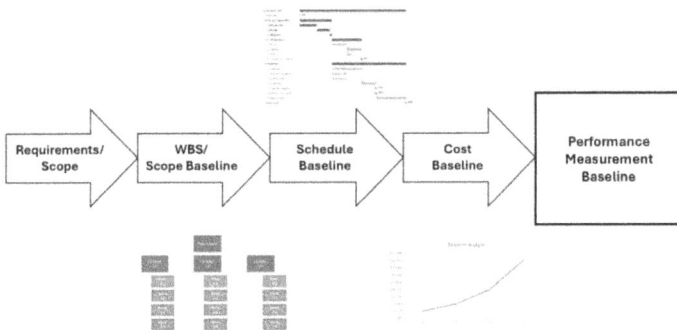

Exhibit 6.1, Journey to the PMB

We will start the journey by examining the scope processes that lead to the development of the scope baseline. The scope baseline is composed of the Project Scope Statement, the

Work Breakdown Structure (WBS), and the WBS dictionary.

The scope planning processes to arrive at the Scope Baseline as promoted by PMI® are the Collect Requirements, Define Scope, and Create WBS processes.

## Collect Requirements

Project success is dependent on gathering and clarifying the requirements for meeting project expectations. The process of collecting requirements is important to the scope baseline because requirements serve as the foundation for scope definition. Think of it this way: the requirements serve as the wish list whereas the scope defines which of those wishes will be realized.

Requirements Come From Stakeholders

Stakeholders are key to defining the requirements of the project to support the project goals and objectives. Achieving successful project outcomes and results is directly related to the clarification and quality of the project requirements.

Soliciting project requirements from stakeholders can often be challenging, especially for large complex projects. For this reason, various tools and techniques are promoted for obtaining, documenting, and prioritizing project requirements.

Tools and Techniques for Gathering Requirements

As we review the various tools and techniques used to gather requirements, consider the items in this list as tools in a toolbox.

The nature and specific objectives of the project will determine which tools or techniques are better suited for the project.

The following list describes some of the more commonly used tools and techniques:

- Facilitated workshops – These workshops are facilitated by the project manager or other designated facilitator. The purpose of the workshops is to solicit requirements and organize them for requirements documentation. The workshops should be organized to respect the time and input from each stakeholder attending the workshop. Multiple workshops may be required when there are too many stakeholders to be effectively facilitated in one session. These workshops may require the use of some of the other techniques identified in this list, such as brainstorming and focus groups.

- Brainstorming – Brainstorming is a process of generating ideas. Typically, brainstorming is conducted in several iterations. The first pass or iteration is to generate as many ideas as possible without criticizing the ideas or requirements (anything goes). To identify requirements, a second iteration or pass can be used to discuss, evaluate, and prioritize the ideas or requirements. Multiple iterations may be required to achieve consensus.

- Interviews – Interview stakeholders and experts to collect requirements. The project team will analyze the stakeholder register to determine which stakeholders should be interviewed. The project team should review the stakeholder list to determine those stakeholders who are experts or subject matter experts as the requirements from these individuals may be critical to project success. The team should prepare appropriately before the interviews. The preparation may include preparing a list of questions, analyzing the stakeholders' profiles and needs, and preparing agendas. Interviews can also be used to uncover other stakeholders not already identified who may also contribute to requirements.

- Questionnaires and surveys – When large groups of stakeholders have been identified, questionnaires and surveys can be used to solicit requirements and needs. The project team should invest time in developing the questionnaires and surveys. When responses have been collected, they will be reviewed and analyzed to determine a list of requirements.

- Focus groups – Focus groups can be created when it is more feasible to have representatives from various stakeholder groups participate in a facilitated workshop. Effective facilitation is key to ensuring contributions from the representatives. The representatives should be empowered to represent the interests of the stakeholder groups.

- User stories – Many agile methods promote user stories as a technique to solicit user needs. A facilitator will work with the stakeholders to generate user stories. A user story is intentionally user-focused and not a detailed specification. If properly written, the value of a user story is that it presents the user's need in a form that is easy to use and discuss. Care must be taken to ensure that the facilitator does not introduce bias into the process.

- Observations – Observations are used to obtain knowledge of processes, procedures, or operations from stakeholders. The observations are documented and analyzed to determine requirements. Team members may directly observe a stakeholder or expert perform a process or procedure. This technique is known as "job shadowing." The technique known as "reverse shadowing" is when the stakeholder or expert observes the project team member perform the job.

- Prototypes and storyboards – A prototype is a model used to obtain early feedback from stakeholders on a concept. Prototypes can save cost and time in the long run and can be useful for determining an early go/no-go for a concept. Storyboarding is a form of a prototype to visually represent a series of steps in a process. Feedback from stakeholders is used to determine new requirements or changes to existing requirements.

Prioritizing Requirements

Not all requirements are equal. Prioritizing requirements is important because the project will often focus on the high-priority requirements. Low-priority items may be dropped from the scope of the project due to budget or time restrictions. The following are some methods and techniques used to prioritize requirements:

- MoSCoW technique – this technique is used by the project team to rank requirements. The "M" in MoSCoW represents the "must have" requirements. The little "o" is just a filler and does not represent a category. The "S" represents the "should have" requirements. The "C" represents the "could have" category. The second little "o" does not represent a category. The "W" represents the "won't have" category, unless a case can be built for the requirements to be included but even so, requirements in this category will be lower in priority.

- Kano model – the Kano model is a technique used to rank requirements for a product. Requirements are organized in the following groups:

  o Basic – the essential features or functions of a product.
  o Performance – features or functions that enhance the performance of a product.
  o Excitement – features or functions that enhance the product and generate interest by the consumers.
  o Indifferent – features or functions that are of little or no interest to the consumers of the product.
  o Reverse – features or functions that may cause dissatisfaction by the consumers of the product.

- Paired comparison – this technique is used to rank requirements two at a time until all requirements have been ranked. This technique is more effective for a smaller group of requirements.
- 100 points method – this technique allows the participants to rank requirements by spending up to 100 points on requirements. After all participants have spent their 100 points, the points are totaled, and the requirements can be ranked by points.

Documentation

After all requirements have been collected and ranked, they will be documented in a document known as the requirements documentation or requirements register. This documentation or register will be used to track the requirements through the project phases.

Summary

Defining requirements for a project is a key step in project management, as it ensures that the needs and expectations of stakeholders are understood and aligned with the project's objectives. Properly gathering and documenting requirements not only helps in defining the scope but also serves as a reference throughout the project's phases, reducing misunderstandings and minimizing the risk of missing critical deliverables. This process fosters stakeholder buy-in, facilitates prioritization, and supports decision-making, ultimately contributing to the delivery of successful project outcomes that satisfy all parties involved.

**Define Scope**

The process of defining scope involves transforming the documented requirements into a detailed project scope statement. This statement specifies what the project will deliver, sets acceptance criteria, and clarifies what is included and excluded, forming the foundation for the scope baseline.

The project scope statement is a critical document that translates the requirements into specific deliverables, detailing what the project will accomplish while setting clear acceptance criteria. By precisely delineating scope inclusions and exclusions, it ensures that all stakeholders have a shared understanding of the project's boundaries and objectives.

Components

The components of a project scope statement include:

- Product scope description: Describes the characteristics of the product, service, or result identified in the project charter and elaborated through the requirements.
- Deliverables: Specifies the project's intended outputs and the criteria required for their acceptance. Deliverables can be classified as project deliverables or product deliverables. Project deliverables are typically used for the benefit of the project team when developing the outcomes of the project. Project deliverables are typically created during the execution of the project. Product deliverables are the final products, services, or results delivered to the customer.
- Acceptance Criteria: Outlines the conditions that must be met for deliverables to be approved.
- Scope Exclusions: Clearly identifies what is outside the scope of the project to avoid misunderstandings.

These components collectively ensure clarity, alignment, and a shared understanding among stakeholders.

Benefits

The benefits of having a well-documented and detailed project scope statement include (but are not limited to):

- Providing a clear understanding of the requirements for the benefit of the project team and the stakeholders.
- Framing what is included in the scope of the project versus the exclusions.

- Providing the foundation for additional planning and for iterative development of the scope, if needed.
- Presenting the deliverables of the project which evolved from the analysis of the requirements.
- Obtaining confirmation of the acceptance criteria for the deliverables of the project.

The Project Charter versus the Project Scope Statement

If the project charter identifies the scope of the project, how does the project scope statement differ from the charter? While the project charter does address the scope of the project and may also indicate scope exclusions, it does so at a summary level. The project scope statement presents the scope at a detailed level. It also clearly identifies the detailed deliverables and the acceptance criteria.

Can a team use the Project Charter as the Project Scope Statement? While this may work for a very small project, on larger projects, the two documents serve very different purposes. The project charter is intended to seek approval of the project and presents information for the decision makers that go beyond scope such as high-level costs, project approach, high-level schedule, and key stakeholders. The Project Scope Statement focuses on only the scope and deliverables of the project.

Summary

A well-documented project scope statement is a critical tool in project management as it provides a detailed framework for understanding the project's requirements, deliverables, exclusions, and acceptance criteria. Unlike the project charter, which offers a high-level overview of the project and seeks approval from decision-makers by including costs, schedules, and key stakeholders, the scope statement delves into specifics. It clearly defines the project and product deliverables, outlines acceptance criteria from the customer's perspective, and identifies exclusions to avoid misunderstandings. By offering clarity and focus, the project scope statement ensures alignment among the team and stakeholders, serves as a foundation for further planning, and helps manage expectations, making it invaluable for the successful execution and control of projects.

**Create the Work Breakdown Structure (WBS)**

The process of creating a Work Breakdown Structure (WBS) not only develops a WBS and a WBS dictionary but it also integrates the project scope document to develop the scope baseline.

Once you have defined the scope of work and developed the project scope statement document, you are ready to build the scope baseline. The scope baseline, once approved, provides the basis for controlling the scope of the project.

Components of the Scope Baseline

The scope baseline is composed of the Project Scope Statement, the work breakdown structure (WBS), and the WBS dictionary.

The Project Scope Statement is developed during scope definition. This document details the project scope, defines the deliverables of the project, and specifies exclusions from the project scope.

The WBS and the WBS dictionary are developed after the scope has been agreed. The WBS is a hierarchical structure of the work required to complete the scope of work for the project.

The WBS dictionary provides detailed information to describe the components of the WBS. This detailed information may include activities required to complete the work packages, schedule information, assumptions and constraints, cost estimates, acceptance criteria, and any other detailed information that describes the work to be performed.

Foundation

The scope baseline becomes the foundation for project planning. The scope baseline is a direct input to the scheduling and budget planning processes. It is also used to guide all other planning activities. The scope baseline will become a component of the Performance Measurement Baseline (PMB) and the Integrated Project Management Plan.

Change Control

Once the scope baseline has been approved, it should only be changed through formal change control.

Scope Control

The scope baseline should be monitored throughout the project cycle. It is used to determine variance from the agreed scope. Project performance reports may indicate variances in the schedule and budget objectives. The root cause of the variances may be a deviation from the scope baseline.

The Work Breakdown Structure (WBS)

A work breakdown structure (WBS) is a hierarchical tool used to organize and define the scope of a project. It breaks down the project deliverables into smaller, manageable components, focusing on nouns rather than verbs to emphasize deliverables over activities. A well-structured WBS helps confirm project scope, improve communication with stakeholders, and provides a foundation for scheduling and budgeting. It adheres to the "100% rule," ensuring all work is represented while maintaining simplicity for efficient management.

Seven Steps

Consider these seven steps to create an effective work breakdown structure:

#1: **Decompose** the work of the project into smaller chunks. Start with your project objectives and/or major deliverables identified in your project charter and scope documents. Ask: how can we break these down into "bite-size" chunks?

#2: **Think** nouns (deliverables) of the project, not verbs (activities). Instead of "build a table" (activity), use "Table" as your work package. This allows your WBS to focus on the scope of the project and not on the schedule of the project. The schedule will come together easier if you develop a solid WBS.

#3: **Structure** the deliverables into groupings that make sense for your project. The value of having a solid structure for your WBS is that it makes it easier to understand the overall scope of the project and leads to better scheduling and budgeting.

#4: **Decide** whether you want to group your deliverables by phase or by major deliverables. If your project lends itself to sequential phases (i.e. Concept, Design, Build, and Deliver), you may want to organize your WBS by phase. If your project is better managed by major deliverables, features, or functions (i.e. Facilities, Procurement, Technology, Sales, etc.), you may want to consider a non-phased approach.

#5: **Consider** the "size" of your work packages (the lowest level of your WBS). If the work packages are too large, this makes it difficult to manage your project effectively. If the work packages are too small, this could lead to confusion and unnecessary oversight. My personal preference is to keep the work package size between 40 and 80 hours of work.

#6: **Simplify** the overall WBS. Instead of 50-60 work packages, try 15-20 work packages. Although achieving this level of simplification is more an "art" than a "science" and can be challenging, it is worth the effort and focus. Simplifying the WBS makes communicating the scope of the project much easier.

#7: **Ensure** that all the work of the project is represented by the WBS. PMI® promotes the 100% rule. All the work of the project should be represented by your WBS. This does not mean you need to include all the detail but that detail should be represented within the context of your WBS.

*Examples*

We will review three WBS examples supporting the same project objective. The project objective (high-level scope) is to implement a Project Management Office (PMO) from the ground up. The difference in the three examples is the overall project approach. Example one (Exhibit 6.2) approaches the project through a series of phases. Example two (Exhibit 6.3) organizes the project by types of deliverables, and example three (Exhibit 6.4) assumes that the work will be contracted out to multiple vendors and then organizes the work by vendor.

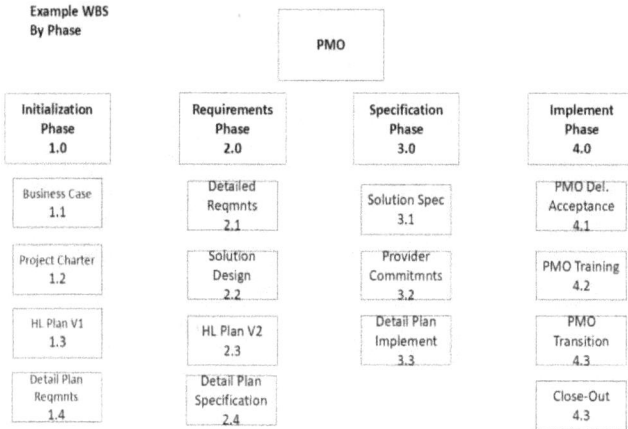

Example WBS
By Phase

PMO

| Initialization Phase 1.0 | Requirements Phase 2.0 | Specification Phase 3.0 | Implement Phase 4.0 |
|---|---|---|---|
| Business Case 1.1 | Detailed Reqmnts 2.1 | Solution Spec 3.1 | PMO Del. Acceptance 4.1 |
| Project Charter 1.2 | Solution Design 2.2 | Provider Commitmnts 3.2 | PMO Training 4.2 |
| HL Plan V1 1.3 | HL Plan V2 2.3 | Detail Plan Implement 3.3 | PMO Transition 4.3 |
| Detail Plan Reqmnts 1.4 | Detail Plan Specification 2.4 | | Close-Out 4.3 |

Exhibit 6.2: WBS Example 1

In this first example, the WBS is organized by phase. The control accounts for this example are the Initialization Phase (1.0), the Requirements Phase (2.0), the Specification Phase (3.0), and the Implement Phase (4.0). This structure is representative of the approach to implement the PMO by completing a series of phases. The Initialization Phase would be completed first and is a prerequisite to starting the

Requirements Phase. Once the Requirements Phase is complete, the project will continue on to the Specification Phase and once the Specification Phase is complete, the project will move on to the last phase, the Implementation Phase. This type of project organization also lends itself to a "rolling wave" level of detail where the first phase will be very detailed and future phases will be less detailed until the work begins on those phases.

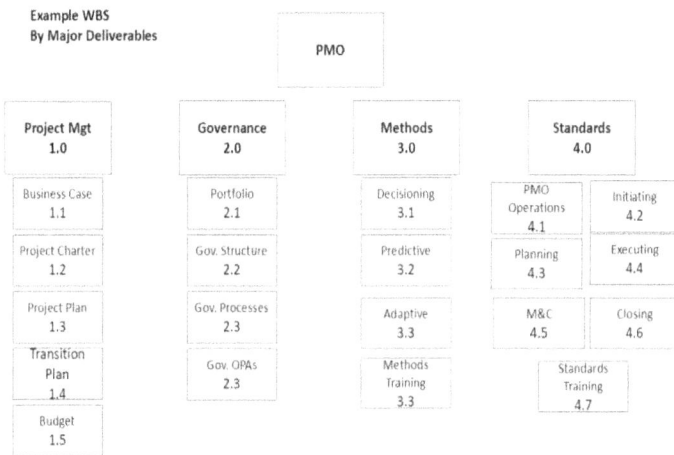

Example WBS
By Major Deliverables

| PMO | | | |
|---|---|---|---|
| **Project Mgt** 1.0 | **Governance** 2.0 | **Methods** 3.0 | **Standards** 4.0 |
| Business Case 1.1 | Portfolio 2.1 | Decisioning 3.1 | PMO Operations 4.1 | Initiating 4.2 |
| Project Charter 1.2 | Gov. Structure 2.2 | Predictive 3.2 | Planning 4.3 | Executing 4.4 |
| Project Plan 1.3 | Gov. Processes 2.3 | Adaptive 3.3 | M&C 4.5 | Closing 4.6 |
| Transition Plan 1.4 | Gov. OPAs 2.3 | Methods Training 3.3 | Standards Training 4.7 | |
| Budget 1.5 | | | |

Exhibit 6.3: WBS Example 2

In example 2, while the high-level scope is the same as in the previous example (implement a PMO), the approach is different. This WBS example is a WBS organized by major deliverables. The control accounts in this example are Project Management (1.0), Governance (2.0), Methods (3.0), and Standards (4.0). Note that this is not a phased approach to the project. The control groups are not dependent on each other. This approach might be preferred when the deliverables are clearly understood and phasing is not required to obtain additional detail. This approach may also be easier to communicate to the project decision makers and the stakeholders.

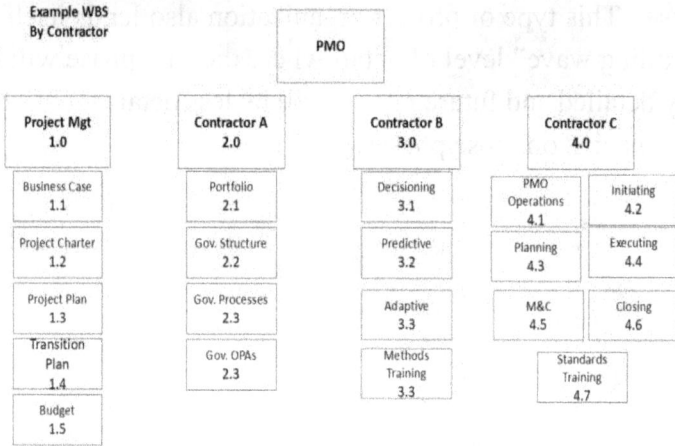

Example WBS
By Contractor

| | PMO | | |
|---|---|---|---|
| Project Mgt 1.0 | Contractor A 2.0 | Contractor B 3.0 | Contractor C 4.0 |

| Project Mgt 1.0 | Contractor A 2.0 | Contractor B 3.0 | Contractor C 4.0 | |
|---|---|---|---|---|
| Business Case 1.1 | Portfolio 2.1 | Decisioning 3.1 | PMO Operations 4.1 | Initiating 4.2 |
| Project Charter 1.2 | Gov. Structure 2.2 | Predictive 3.2 | Planning 4.3 | Executing 4.4 |
| Project Plan 1.3 | Gov. Processes 2.3 | Adaptive 3.3 | M&C 4.5 | Closing 4.6 |
| Transition Plan 1.4 | Gov. OPAs 2.3 | Methods Training 3.3 | Standards Training 4.7 | |
| Budget 1.5 | | | | |

Exhibit 6.4: WBS Example 3

In example 3, the high-level scope is the same as in the others (implement a PMO) but the approach represented by this WBS is different. In this approach, the work is divided into groupings which can be contracted out. This approach will use three vendors to perform the work of the project. The control account for Project Management (1.0) is for overall management of the project, which in this example, will be performed by the general contractor. The Tools - Vendor A (2.0) represents the work that will be performed by Vendor A. Methods – Vendor B (3.0) represents work to be performed by Vendor B. And Standards – Vendor C (4.0) represents work to be performed by Vendor C. As you can see from this example, the work is organized by function and assigned to the vendors best fit for those functions.

This completes our review of three examples of WBS with a similar high-level scope but with different implementation approaches. The WBS structure organization is flexible and can help a team consider different ways to organize the work in a project.

Benefits of a WBS

What are the benefits of using a WBS? Consider this starter list:

- Clarifies the work of the project.
- Supports the 100% rule (defines all the work of the project, not more, and not less).
- Provides a visual mapping of the work to be performed.
- Provides a crucial component of the scope baseline.
- Provides the structure for organizing the activities of the project.
- Provides the foundation for determining the project budget.
- Provides a foundation for planning.
- Helps prevent scope creep (unnecessary and unauthorized scope changes).
- Facilitates communication and collaboration with the team and stakeholders.
- Provides a basis for estimating resources, schedules, and costs.
- Facilitates mentoring of new team members and stakeholders.

WBS Dictionary

The WBS Dictionary serves to support the Work Breakdown Structure (WBS), offering detailed descriptions of each component within the project. It provides critical information such as deliverables, activities, resources, and timelines associated with each element of the WBS. By documenting this data systematically, the WBS Dictionary ensures clarity and alignment among team members and stakeholders, reducing misunderstandings and enhancing overall project efficiency. As a vital part of the scope baseline, it not only supports accurate planning and execution but also aids in maintaining control over scope changes, thereby safeguarding the project's objectives.

Summary

The "Create WBS" process creates the scope baseline. The scope baseline is a critical element in project planning, comprising the Scope Statement, Work Breakdown Structure (WBS), and the WBS Dictionary. By providing clear boundaries for what falls within the project's objectives, the scope baseline prevents scope creep and ensures that all efforts align with the established goals. Additionally, it serves as a foundation for estimating schedules, budgets, and resource requirements, thereby enhancing precision in planning. The scope baseline also facilitates communication and collaboration among team members and stakeholders.

## Develop the Schedule

The process of developing the schedule creates another component of the Performance Measurement Baseline (PMB), the Schedule Baseline.

In this section, we will explore a simple step-by-step process of developing a project schedule. We will also provide a definition of the critical path and the importance of this concept for scheduling. We will also provide some guidance for selecting a scheduling tool.

A Seven Step Process to Developing a Schedule

Consider these seven steps when developing a schedule to keep your project on track::

#1: Start with the Scope documents (Scope Statement, WBS, and WBS dictionary). "Decompose" the scope into activities. Although this seems counterintuitive, it is much more effective than just brainstorming the activities of the project and then organizing the activities. An effective WBS will provide the structure and will guide the team to the 100% rule. All activities should support the scope baseline.

#2: Add milestones to the activity list. Milestones help mark progress through the project. A milestone is not an activity. It is a point in time, a marker. A milestone has no work or duration associated with it. Milestones are commonly used to mark the completion of key events in the project. If the project work is managed through phases, consider a milestone for the completion of each phase. The "art" of adding milestones is ensuring you don't have too many or too few.

#3: Consider "rolling wave" planning. Rolling wave planning can be used with a phased approach when it may be difficult to define the activities for future phases. Detail planning will occur when the next phase begins.

#4: Sequence the activities of the project to optimize the project timeline. Every activity should have a predecessor (the "driver") and a successor (the "dependent" activity). The following sequencing techniques provide variety to the scheduling:

- Finish to Start (most common): the predecessor's finish determines the start of the successor activity
- Start to Start: the predecessor's start determines the start of the successor activity
- Finish to Finish: the predecessor's finish determines the finish of the successor activity
- Start to Finish (least common): the predecessor's start determines the finish of the successor activity
- Leads and lags: a lead is an acceleration of the successor activity. A lag is a planned delay of the successor activity.

#5: Estimate the durations of the activities by taking into account the resources performing the work and using various estimating techniques such as:

- Analogous (least accurate) – based on a high-level benchmark or reference; sometimes called "top-down."
- Parametric – driven by a parameter (i.e. square footage, number of units, etc.).
- Definitive – driven by the lowest level of detail (also called "bottom-up")
- Three-point estimating – strives for more realistic estimates by averaging the Optimistic, Pessimistic, and Most Likely estimates. The PERT estimating technique weighs the most likely estimate by four.

#6: Determine the critical path of the project. The critical path of the project is the longest path of activities that determines the earliest project finish date. Activities on the critical path have no slack or "project float" meaning any delay of these activities will delay the project. For small projects, the critical path can usually be determined manually. For larger projects, a project management tool is typically used to determine the activities on the critical path. A time reserve or contingency may also be added to the baseline to allow for 'known unknowns" in the project timeline.

#7: Baseline the schedule once planning has been completed. A baseline is the approved version of the schedule which remains "frozen" until formally changed. The "live" schedule is compared against the baseline to determine variance. Proper project management practice requires formal change approval to modify the baseline.

Consider these seven tips for building your schedule during the planning process.

We will now explore the concept of the critical path, an important concept in scheduling.

Critical Path

The critical path methodology analyzes the schedule to determine the sequence of activities that define the earliest project completion. The critical path on a project schedule is the longest path that determines the earliest project completion. Any delay in any activity on the critical path will delay the project's completion.

Steps Required to Determine the Critical Path

The following are the steps required to determine the critical path:

- Decompose the work breakdown structure to define all the activities of the project.
- Identify the dependencies of all the activities. Every activity should have a predecessor and a successor.
- Once the dependencies have been established, create a network diagram of all the activities in the schedule. Exhibit 6.5 illustrates a simple precedence diagram, also known as a PDM:

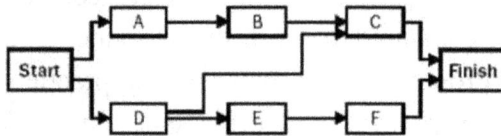

Exhibit 6.5: Example PDM

- Estimate the durations for all the activities in the schedule.
- Determine the critical path (or the longest path) in the schedule. See Exhibit 6.6 for a simple example.

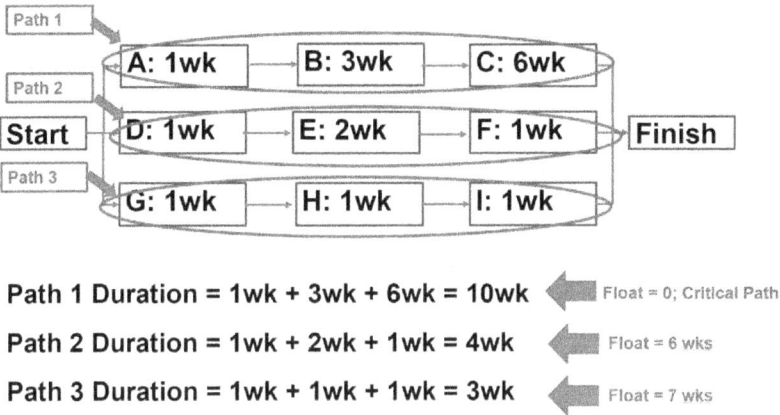

Path 1

| A: 1wk | → | B: 3wk | → | C: 6wk |

Path 2

| Start | D: 1wk | → | E: 2wk | → | F: 1wk | → | Finish |

Path 3

| G: 1wk | → | H: 1wk | → | I: 1wk |

**Path 1 Duration = 1wk + 3wk + 6wk = 10wk**   ⬅ Float = 0; Critical Path

**Path 2 Duration = 1wk + 2wk + 1wk = 4wk**   ⬅ Float = 6 wks

**Path 3 Duration = 1wk + 1wk + 1wk = 3wk**   ⬅ Float = 7 wks

Exhibit 6.6: Example Critical Path

In this example, the critical path is Path 1, which at 10 weeks long is the longest path in the schedule.

- Calculate the schedule flexibility or float for each path. The float or amount of flexibility on the critical path will be zero. There is no schedule flexibility on the critical path. Any delay on the critical path will delay the project. In this example, the amount of project float for Path 2 is six weeks (calculated by subtracting the duration of Path 2 from the duration of Path 1). The amount of float on Path 3 is seven weeks (calculated by subtracting the duration of Path 3 from the duration of Path 1).

Managing the Critical Path

Now that we have determined the critical path for the project, how do we use this to manage the schedule? We will use the critical path example above to demonstrate two situations:

- **Situation 1:** The team member working on Activity B reports that he will be a week late. Since Activity B is on Path 1 which is the critical path, this delay will impact the project completion unless we take some action. One possible action could be to add a resource to help complete Activity B within the three-week duration and prevent delaying the project. Another action could be to reduce the duration of Activity C by one week to make up for the delay in Activity B. The duration of Activity C can be reduced by adding resources.
- **Situation 2:** Activity F is delayed by two weeks. Activity F is on Path 2 and Path 2 has six weeks of float. In this situation, no action is required as there is six weeks of float on Path 2. Activity F can be delayed by two weeks without impacting the project completion date.

The critical path methodology provides visibility to all the activities on the project and allows you to monitor the critical path for any delay. Any activity delay should be analyzed to determine impacts to the schedule. Significant delay on a non-critical path activity can also be a problem and may create a new critical path.

Advantages

The advantages of the critical path method are:

- Allows for clearer communication regarding schedule management.

- Allows the team to focus on the activities most likely to cause delay to the schedule.
- Improves management of schedule risk.
- Improves accuracy of scheduling.
- Allows the project manager to take corrective and preventive actions to prevent project schedule delays.

Disadvantages

The disadvantages of the critical path method are:

- High complexity, especially on a project with a significant number of activities.
- Poor estimating can impact the critical path determination.
- High float activities may not be monitored closely.
- Resource constraints are not taken into consideration.

Summary of Critical Path

The critical path methodology can be used to determine the critical path of the project. Any delay on the critical path may delay the project. The schedule can then be managed to ensure that the appropriate actions are taken when there are any delays to activities on the critical path.

Scheduling Tools

Scheduling tools are instrumental for project managers in ensuring the timely completion of projects. They allow project managers to determine the critical path of a project, which highlights activities that directly impact the project timeline. By identifying the critical path, delays in key tasks can be managed more effectively, and corrective or preventive actions can be taken promptly. Scheduling tools also provide visibility into the sequence of activities, dependencies, and float times, aiding in the prioritization of tasks.

When selecting a scheduling tool, project managers should consider the following factors:

- Complexity of the Project: Ensure the tool can handle projects with numerous activities and dependencies.
- Resource Management Capabilities: Select a tool that accounts for resource constraints and optimizes resource allocation.
- Ease of Use: Choose a tool that is user-friendly and fits the skill level of the team using it.
- Integration with Other Systems: Consider tools that integrate seamlessly with budgeting, risk management, and communication platforms.
- Reporting Features: Choose tools that provide clear and customizable reports to track progress and highlight potential delays.

These considerations ensure that the chosen tool not only supports accurate scheduling but also aligns with the overall project management framework.

A scheduling tool can also provide a Gantt chart (see Exhibit 6.7). A Gantt chart is a powerful visual tool that provides a graphical representation of a project schedule. It allows project managers to see the timing and duration of each task alongside their dependencies. Each task is displayed as a horizontal bar, spanning across a timeline that indicates the start and end dates. This format enables easy identification of critical activities, tracking progress, and spotting potential delays. By presenting these details in a clear and intuitive layout, Gantt charts help teams manage resources, synchronize efforts, and ensure alignment with project goals, making them indispensable for effective planning and execution.

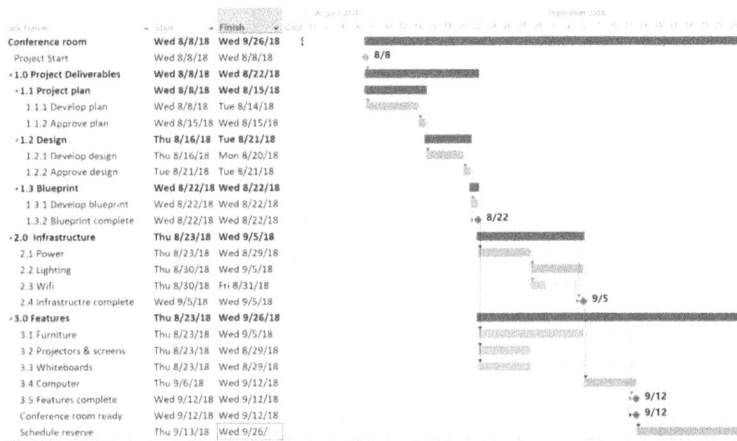

| Task Name | Start | Finish |
| --- | --- | --- |
| Conference room | Wed 8/8/18 | Wed 9/26/18 |
| Project Start | Wed 8/8/18 | Wed 8/8/18 |
| 1.0 Project Deliverables | Wed 8/8/18 | Wed 8/22/18 |
| 1.1 Project plan | Wed 8/8/18 | Wed 8/15/18 |
| 1.1.1 Develop plan | Wed 8/8/18 | Tue 8/14/18 |
| 1.1.2 Approve plan | Wed 8/15/18 | Wed 8/15/18 |
| 1.2 Design | Thu 8/16/18 | Tue 8/21/18 |
| 1.2.1 Develop design | Thu 8/16/18 | Mon 8/20/18 |
| 1.2.2 Approve design | Tue 8/21/18 | Tue 8/21/18 |
| 1.3 Blueprint | Wed 8/22/18 | Wed 8/22/18 |
| 1.3.1 Develop blueprint | Wed 8/22/18 | Wed 8/22/18 |
| 1.3.2 Blueprint complete | Wed 8/22/18 | Wed 8/22/18 |
| 2.0 Infrastructure | Thu 8/23/18 | Wed 9/5/18 |
| 2.1 Power | Thu 8/23/18 | Wed 8/29/18 |
| 2.2 Lighting | Thu 8/30/18 | Wed 9/5/18 |
| 2.3 Wifi | Thu 8/30/18 | Fri 8/31/18 |
| 2.4 Infrastructre complete | Wed 9/5/18 | Wed 9/5/18 |
| 3.0 Features | Thu 8/23/18 | Wed 9/26/18 |
| 3.1 Furniture | Thu 8/23/18 | Wed 9/5/18 |
| 3.2 Projectors & screens | Thu 8/23/18 | Wed 8/29/18 |
| 3.3 Whiteboards | Thu 8/23/18 | Wed 8/29/18 |
| 3.4 Computer | Thu 9/6/18 | Wed 9/12/18 |
| 3.5 Features complete | Wed 9/12/18 | Wed 9/12/18 |
| Conference room ready | Wed 9/12/18 | Wed 9/12/18 |
| Schedule reserve | Thu 9/13/18 | Wed 9/26/ |

Exhibit 6.7: Example Gantt Chart

## Summary

Building a project schedule involves identifying tasks, estimating their durations, and outlining dependencies to create a logical sequence of activities. The critical path, which represents the longest sequence of dependent tasks, determines the minimum project duration and highlights tasks that cannot afford delays. When choosing a scheduling tool, project managers should evaluate factors such as complexity handling, resource management capabilities, ease of use, integration with other systems, and robust reporting features to ensure alignment with project goals and efficient execution.

**Determine the Project Budget**

Determining a project budget is simple…if you know your costs. And you know your work. And you know what activities are required to complete the work. And you know what resources you need. And you know the costs of your resources. And you have proven estimating techniques.

Consider these seven steps to determine a budget for your project.

**#1: Start with the scope and schedule documents**. The Work Breakdown Structure (WBS) will provide the organizational structure for aggregating costs into control accounts. The schedule provides the detailed activities of the project along with estimated resources required to perform the work of the project.

**#2: Estimate the costs of the project** by evaluating the costs of the detailed activities of the project. Depending on the level of detail available, estimating techniques can include Analogous (top-down or "educated guess"), Parametric, Definitive (bottom-up), and three-point estimating. In addition, seek the help of experts and use historical information from past projects.

**#3: Aggregate the detailed costs of the project into Control Accounts** (defined in the WBS). The sum of the Control Accounts is equal to the total project estimates (before adding a contingency reserve).

**#4: Add a contingency reserve** to the total project estimates. A contingency reserve allows for anticipated variances in costs ("known unknowns"). A contingency reserve can be determined using standard guidelines such as a standard percentage of the costs or may be determined by the analysis of project risks.

**#5: Create a cost baseline** for the project. The cost baseline is the time-phased budget for the project. The total planned spend for the project is the total of the project estimates plus the contingency reserve. Cost performance is measured against the cost baseline. The cost baseline can be graphically displayed with an S-curve (see exhibit 6.8). Once the cost baseline has been approved, it should only be modified through approved changes.

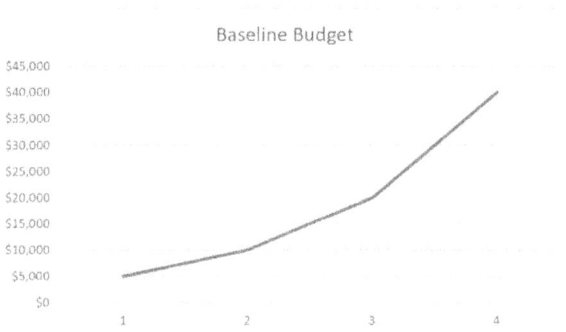

Baseline Budget

Exhibit 6.8: Example S-Curve

**#6: Determine the overall project budget** by adding the management reserve which is determined by management to cover uncertain events ("unknown unknowns") which may impact the project costs. The management reserve is NOT included in the project cost performance baseline. Use of the management reserve requires management approval.

**#7: Reconcile the Project Budget** against the scope and the project timeline. If the project budget is considered "too high," reconsider the scope of the project. If the timeline is "too long," consider increasing the budget.

While larger projects may require a greater investment of time and expertise (call your favorite accountant), these seven tips guide you in the right direction to determining a project budget.

Once you have determined the overall budget, then you can consider the project's approach to funding the project.

The budgeting process for a project involves several key steps, starting with the scope and schedule documents to define the structure and activities of the project. Costs are estimated using various techniques, including analogous, parametric, and bottom-up approaches, often with input from experts and historical data. These detailed costs are then aggregated into Control Accounts, forming the total project estimates before adding a contingency reserve for anticipated variances. A cost baseline is created, incorporating the contingency reserve, to serve as the time-phased budget for measuring cost performance. An additional management reserve is added for unforeseen events, requiring management approval for use. Finally, the project budget is reconciled against the project scope and timeline, adjusting as necessary to ensure feasibility and alignment with objectives.

## Performance Measurement Baseline

To complete the building of the performance measurement baseline, control accounts need to be established, and each control account must be assigned to an organizational team or individual for management. Control accounts are defined as management control points where scope, schedule and budget, and actual costs are integrated and then used in earned value for performance measurement.

A responsibility assignment matrix can be used to illustrate the assignment of control accounts to team or individuals. In the simple example demonstrated in Exhibit 6.9, you can see that Team 3 is responsible for control accounts 1.1 and 2.1.

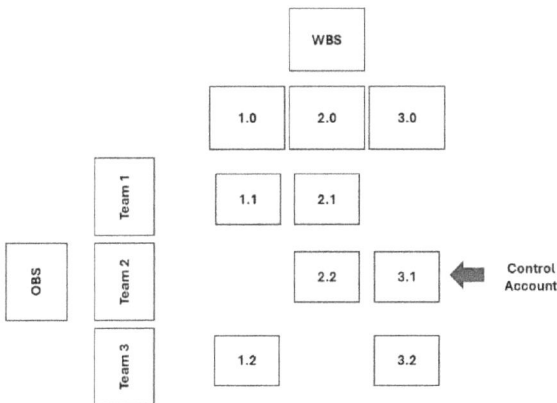

Exhibit 6.9, Example RAM

The teams or individuals responsible for each control account will develop a control account plan. The control account plan (CAP) is the detailed plan for a control account. This plan includes the manager responsible, the detailed scope of work to be performed, the schedule and any relevant milestones, and the budget. The use of control account plans provides for tighter control over project performance.

A Performance Measurement Baseline (PMB) is considered complete and ready to be used for earned value management when the following have been completed:

- All work and planning packages have been estimated and budgeted. Work packages have well defined work while planning packages may be used for future work which has not yet been clearly defined.
- Risks have been identified, and risk responses or strategies have been considered. Risks may directly affect the contingency amounts built into the budget.
- All work and planning packages have been scheduled.
- All control accounts have been assigned to a team or person.
- Methods for measuring earned value have been determined.
- Performance measurement methods have been determined.
- The process is in place to capture actual costs and work completion.

In summary, the performance measurement baseline is developed in planning and is used to measure project performance. This baseline includes contingency reserve but does not include management reserve. The performance measurement baseline will be managed through control accounts which have been assigned to teams or individuals. Accountability can be established through a responsibility assignment matrix.

Once the performance measurement baseline has been established, work needs to be authorized. The authorization for the work is outlined here:

- The project manager receives authorization to begin work on the project (typically through a project charter).
- The project manager authorizes the control account managers to begin work on the assigned work packages.
- The control account managers authorize specific individuals to begin work on the tasks for the control account. The control account managers ensure the proper charging of time or accrual of costs to the control account.
- After the work has been authorized, changes to the work or control account are controlled through the change control procedures.

**Takeaways and a Prompt List**

The key takeaways from this chapter include the following:

- The scope baseline serves as the foundation of the Performance Measurement Baseline (PMB).
- The schedule baseline which is driven by the critical path determines the measurement timeline.
- The cost baseline determines the time-phased budget for the project.
- The sequential series of processes (collect requirements, define scope, create WBS, develop the schedule, and determine budget) lead to the creation of the Performance Measurement Baseline.

Consider the following prompt list of questions as you consider the implementation of EVM for your project or organization:

- Do your project managers and project teams understand the concept of the Performance Measurement Baseline (PMB)?
- Are PMBs created for your larger projects?
- If your organization does not promote the creation of a performance measurement baseline, can the organization benefit from using this concept to better plan and control projects?

# Chapter 7

# Preparing the Project for EVM

Effective earned value management is dependent on a clearly defined performance measurement baseline (PMB). As you are starting a contract project to be controlled by earned value management, it is important to understand the components of the contract. Let us take a look at a project contract from an EVM perspective:

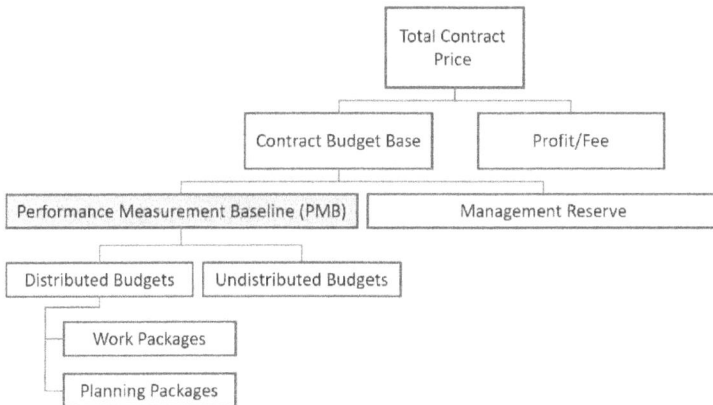

Exhibit 7.1: Total Contract Price

The total contract price is the negotiated contract price for the project. The total contract price includes the profit or fee. The profit or fee is not considered for performance measurement. The contract budget base is managed by the organization performing the work of the project.

Notice that the contract budget base includes the management reserve. The management reserve is tightly controlled and can only be used through the authorization of a change request. The management reserve is typically set aside for unexpected work which may come up during the course of the project. The management reserve is not included in the performance measurement baseline..

The performance measurement baseline is managed by the project manager. This baseline will be used to monitor the performance of the project. The PMB is organized into distributed budgets and undistributed budgets. Distributed budgets are those budgets that have been allocated to control accounts and can include budgets for work packages (near term work) and planning packages (longer term work). Distributed budgets include contingency reserves.

Undistributed budgets have not yet been assigned to control accounts. Undistributed budget applies to work that has been authorized but has not been assigned to a control account manager.

Control accounts can be established at different levels. They can be established for a single work package as in this example illustrated in Exhibit 7.2.

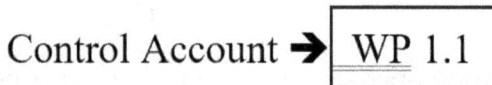

Control Account ➜ WP 1.1

Exhibit 7.2: Control Account for Single WP

Or they can be established at a rollup level as in the example illustrated in Exhibit 7.3.

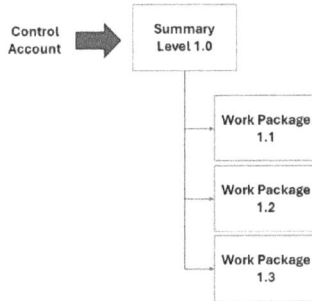

Exhibit 7.3: Control Account for Rollup Level

Factors to be considered in deciding the appropriate number and level of controls accounts include cost of management, level of risk, contract requirements, and management expectations. Having too many control accounts increases the overhead and general management required. Having too few control accounts may lead to increased risk. Let us take a look at an example of a control account at startup (Exhibit 7.4).

Control Account: 1.0 Conference Room Buildout

| WBS # Reference | Activities: | Budget | Week 1 | Week 2 | Week 3 | Week 4 | Week 5 | Week 6 |
|---|---|---|---|---|---|---|---|---|
| 1.1 | Develop project plan | $500 | $550 | | | | | |
| 1.2 | Develop design | $2,100 | | $2,310 | | | | |
| 1.3 | Complete power reqmnts | $1,000 | | | $1,100 | | | |
| 1.4 | Install lighting | $1,500 | | | | $1,100 | $550 | |
| 1.5 | Install Wifi | $300 | | | | $330 | | |
| 1.6 | Acquire furniture | $5,000 | | | $2,750 | $2,750 | | |
| 1.7 | Acquire projectors and screens | $2,000 | | | $2,200 | | | |
| 1.8 | Acquire whiteboards | $500 | | | | $550 | | |
| 1.9 | Acquire computers/printers | $2,000 | | | $1,100 | $1,100 | | |
| 1.10 | Conduct inspections/testing | $1,500 | | | | | | $1,650 |
| | Contingency Reserve | $1,640 | | | | | | |
| | **Cost Baseline** | **$18,040** | | | | | | |
| | Summary Costs | | $550 | $2,310 | $7,150 | $5,830 | $550 | $1,650 |
| | Time-Phased Budget | | $550 | $2,860 | $10,010 | $15,840 | $16,390 | $18,040 |

Time-Phased Budget

$20,000

$15,000

$10,000

$5,000

$0

1    2    3    4    5    6

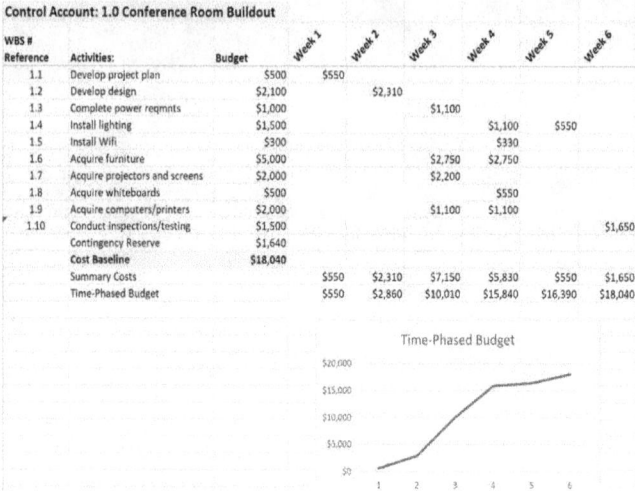

Exhibit 7.4: Sample Control Account

In this example, the total budget to be managed by the control account manager is $18,040. This total includes contingency reserve but does not include a management reserve. Notice that the budget is time-phased. The total amount of $18,040 is also called the Budget at Completion (BAC) for this control account. The control account manager is expected to manage the work within the budget. The contingency reserve may be used for expected variance. If an unexpected situation arises and an additional budget is required to complete the work, the control account manager would have to resolve this situation with the project manager. In some cases, this may require change control to request additional budget from the management reserve.

Clearly defining a performance management baseline along with assigning control accounts to control account managers provides for tighter control over the scope, schedule, and costs for a project. Using the baseline for comparison to actual results can allow for early detection of problems and provide opportunities for corrections and preventive actions.

## Takeaways and a Prompt List

The key takeaways from this chapter include the following:

- The performance measurement baseline (PMB) is managed by the project manager. This baseline will be used to monitor the performance of the project.
- Neither the management reserve or the project profit (fee) is included in the PMB.
- Control accounts can be established at different levels.
- Assigning control accounts to control account managers provides for tighter control over the scope, schedule, and costs for a project.

Consider the following prompt list of questions as you consider the implementation of EVM for your project or organization:

- Are PMBs determined for the major projects in your organization?
- Are control accounts established for major projects in your organization?
- Do project managers in your organization assign control accounts to control account managers?

# Chapter 8

# Measures Required for EVM

To have effective earned value reporting, we need four specific measures:

- Planned Value (PV)
- Actual Cost (AC)
- Earned Value (EV)
- Budget at Completion (BAC)

We will review these in more detail.

### Planned Value (PV)

Planned Value (PV) is defined as "the authorized budget assigned to scheduled work." At a point in time, it is the budget for the work planned to be completed by that time. Let us look at an example of a control account plan (Exhibit 8.1).

Control Account: 1.0 Conference Room Buildout

| WBS # Reference | Activities: | Budget | Week 1 | Week 2 | Week 3 | Week 4 | Week 5 | Week 6 |
|---|---|---|---|---|---|---|---|---|
| 1.1 | Develop project plan | $500 | $550 | | | | | |
| 1.2 | Develop design | $2,100 | | $2,310 | | | | |
| 1.3 | Complete power reqmnts | $1,000 | | | $1,100 | | | |
| 1.4 | Install lighting | $1,500 | | | | $1,100 | $550 | |
| 1.5 | Install Wifi | $300 | | | | $330 | | |
| 1.6 | Acquire furniture | $5,000 | | | $2,750 | $2,750 | | |
| 1.7 | Acquire projectors and screens | $2,000 | | | $2,200 | | | |
| 1.8 | Acquire whiteboards | $500 | | | | $550 | | |
| 1.9 | Acquire computers/printers | $2,000 | | | $1,100 | $1,100 | | |
| 1.10 | Conduct inspections/testing | $1,500 | | | | | | $1,650 |
| | Contingency Reserve | $1,640 | | | | | | |
| | **Cost Baseline** | **$18,040** | | | | | | |
| | Summary Costs | | $550 | $2,310 | $7,150 | $5,830 | $550 | $1,650 |
| | Time-Phased Budget | | $550 | $2,860 | $10,010 | $15,840 | $16,390 | $18,040 |

Time-Phased Budget

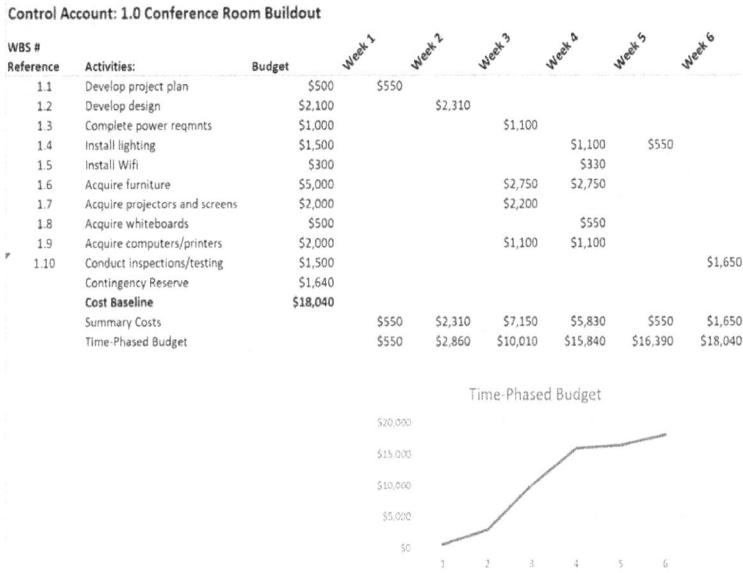

| | |
|---|---|
| $20,000 | |
| $15,000 | |
| $10,000 | |
| $5,000 | |
| $0 | |
| | 1   2   3   4   5   6 |

Exhibit 8.1: Control Account Plan

In this example, the Planned Value for this control account at the end of week three is $10,010, which is the cumulative total of the budget at that time. In other words, $10,010 of work is expected to be complete by the end of week three.

Planned Value is used to determine schedule variance and schedule performance.

## Actual Cost (AC)

Actual cost (AC) is the actual cost incurred for the work performed as of the status date. For most resource driven costs, this should be easy to capture or record. If a resource costing $100 an hour has completed four hours of work on an activity by that reporting date, the actual costs are $400 for that activity.

The costs should not be confused with the invoice or payment and may need to be accrued. For example, if the project used an external trainer for $1,000 in week one, the actual costs are $1,000. The invoice for the training and the payment may occur at different times.

## Earned Value (EV)

Earned Value (EV) is the authorized budget for the work performed as of the status date. During planning, the approach to measuring earned value would have been decided. The earned value measurement method may also vary depending on the type of work to be performed. Additionally, the organization may dictate the measurement method.

We will look at the following six methods for measuring earned value:

- Percent complete
- Fixed formula
- Weighted milestones
- Physical measurement (units complete)
- Apportioned effort
- Level of effort

### Percent Complete

This is a subjective method of determining the amount of work completed. The "percent complete" is determined by the person performing the work or a supervisor of a team performing the work. "Percent complete" can be any value between zero and one hundred.

See this table for an example of earned value calculations using percent complete.

| | Budget at Completion (BAC) | Percent Complete | Earned Value |
|---|---|---|---|
| WP 1 | $10,000 | 90% | $9,000 |
| WP 2 | $5,000 | 30% | $1,500 |
| WP 3 | $7,500 | 10% | $750 |
| Total | $22,500 | | $11,250 |

In this example, the calculated earned value for the three work packages using the "percent complete" method is $11,250.

**Fixed Formula**

The fixed formula measurement method is an objective method as a percentage of the value of the work will be credited when the work begins and the remaining percentage will be credited when the work is complete. Some of the more common fixed formulas are 50/50, 25/75, and 0/100.

See this table for an example of earned value calculations using the 50/50 fixed formula.

| | Budget at Completion (BAC) | Status | Fixed Formula | Earned Value |
|---|---|---|---|---|
| WP 1 | $10,000 | Started | 50/50 | $5,000 |
| WP 2 | $5,000 | Complete | 50/50 | $5,000 |
| WP 3 | $7,500 | Not started | 50/50 | $0 |
| Total | $22,500 | | | $10,000 |

In this example, the calculated earned value for the three work packages using the 50/50 fixed formula is $10,000.

Using the 0/100 fixed formula method requires the work to be completed to get credit for the work. See this table for an example of earned value calculations using the 0/100 fixed formula.

| | Budget at Completion (BAC) | Status | Fixed Formula | Earned Value |
|---|---|---|---|---|
| WP 1 | $10,000 | Started | 0/100 | $0 |
| WP 2 | $5,000 | Complete | 0/100 | $5,000 |
| WP 3 | $7,500 | Not started | 0/100 | $0 |
| Total | $22,500 | | | $5,000 |

In this example, the calculated earned value for the three work packages using the 0/100 fixed formula is $5,000.

**Weighted Milestones**

The weighted milestones method determines the value to be earned based on the completion of milestones. See this table for an example of earned value calculations using the weighted milestone method.

| | Budget at Completion (BAC) | Milestone 1 | Milestone 2 | Milestone 3 | Completed Milestones | Earned Value |
|---|---|---|---|---|---|---|
| WP 1 | $10,000 | $4,000 | $4,000 | $2,000 | All | $10,000 |
| WP 2 | $5,000 | $3,000 | $1,000 | $1,000 | M1, M2 | $4,000 |
| WP 3 | $7,500 | $500 | $3,000 | $4,000 | M1 | $500 |
| Total | $22,500 | | | | | $14,500 |

In this example, each milestone has a value and that value is credited when the milestone has been completed. If a planned milestone is missed, this will lead to an unfavorable variance.

**Units Complete (physical measurement)**

The "units complete" method is a simple method for calculating earned value. If the work lends itself to a physical measurement, the measurement is used to calculate earned value. See this table for an example of earned value calculations using the "units complete" method.

| | Budget at Completion (BAC) | Unit Value | Number of units complete | Earned Value |
|---|---|---|---|---|
| WP 1 | $10,000 | $100 | 40 | $4,000 |
| WP 2 | $5,000 | $50 | 50 | $2,500 |
| WP 3 | $7,500 | $500 | 1 | $500 |
| Total | $22,500 | | | $7,000 |

As you can see in this example, earned value is only credited when a unit has been completed.

**Apportioned Effort**

The "apportioned effort" method of calculating earned value is used to measure value for work performed in support of a discreet work package. This is typically used for administrative or shared support work. For example, project management office support is provided to certain work packages. The earned value for the project management office support is earned based on a stated percentage of the earned value of the work package, perhaps 10%. Continuing this example, if a work package is valued at $10,000 and the work package has earned value of $5,000, then the earned value for the supporting activity (project management office support) will be $500 (10% of $5,000).

## Level of Effort (LOE)

The "level of effort" method of calculating earned value is the least desirable of the various methods but may be appropriate for administrative or management work, which is hard to measure. Earned value is allocated over the time period of the work. Using this method, earned value will always equal the planned value. See this example:

| | Administrative Support | | | |
| --- | --- | --- | --- | --- |
| | M1 | M2 | M3 | M4 |
| Planned Value | $2,000 | $2,000 | $2,000 | $2,000 |
| Earmed Value | $2,000 | $2,000 | | |

EV at end of second period = $4,000

In this example, the total earned value at the end of the second period is $4,000.

## Budget at Completion (BAC)

The budget at completion (BAC) is the total budget for a work package. The sum of all the BACs for the work packages, planning packages and undistributed budgets is the BAC for the project.

**Takeaways and a Prompt List**

The key takeaways from this chapter include the following:

- EVM requires four measures: Planned Value (PV), Actual Costs (AC), Earned Value (EV), and the Budget at Completion (BAC).
- Planned Value (PV) is defined as "the authorized budget assigned to scheduled work."
- Actual cost (AC) is the actual cost incurred for the work performed as of the status date.
- Earned Value (EV) is the authorized budget for the work performed as of the status date.
- There are six methods for calculating earned value: percent complete, fixed formula, weighted milestones, units complete, apportioned effort, and level of effort.

Consider the following prompt list of questions as you consider the implementation of EVM for your project or organization:

- Are the EVM measures understood and used on major projects in your organization?
- Does your organization provide guidelines or standards for determining how to calculate and report earned value?

- Does your organization provide guidelines or standards for determining actual costs?

# Chapter 9

# Performance Formulas

Earned Value Management provides multiple formulas for measuring variance against the performance measurement baseline (PMB). These formulas will help the project manager monitor progress, perform an analysis of team performance, and take corrective and preventive actions.

The formulas use the following key measures:

- Planned value (PV). This is the authorized budget assigned to scheduled work
- Earned value (EV). This is the budget for the work performed.
- Actual cost (AC). This is the realized cost of the work performed.
- Budget at Completion (BAC). This is the sum of all the budgets for the work of the project.

We will review the earned value formulas in three different categories:

- Cost performance
- Schedule performance
- Forecasting

**Cost Performance**

For cost performance, we will review three formulas: cost variance (CV), cost performance index (CPI), and the "to complete performance index" (TCPI).

- **Cost variance (CV).** Using earned value, the cost variance formula will provide an assessment of the costs against the value of the work performed. Consider the following situation: your project has a budget at completion of $100,000. The actual costs are $50,000. If this was the only information you had, you can only determine that you have used fifty percent of your budget. But how much work have you completed for what you have spent? Are you spending as expected? Are you spending more or less? The cost variance formula will provide the answer.

  The cost variance formula is: CV = EV – AC. Cost variance is equal to earned value minus the actual cost.

  Let us apply this formula to the situation above. Before we do, we will need to know the earned value. If we have determined that the earned value is forty thousand dollars, then the cost variance is negative ten thousand dollars, which is the earned value of forty thousand dollars minus the actual costs of fifty thousand dollars. See the formula applied here:

  CV = EV – AC
  CV = $40K - $50K
  CV = $(10K)

The result is negative ten thousand dollars. A negative variance tells us that we are spending more than what we should be spending. A zero variance tells us that we are spending what we should be spending. A positive variance tells us that we are spending less than we have budgeted for the work performed.

- **Cost performance index (CPI).** The cost performance index measures cost efficiency and is used to help determine if the budget at completion will be achieved. Once you have determined the cost efficiency or the CPI, then you should be able to ask: if we continue at this rate, will we complete the project within budget or not?

  The cost performance index formula is: $CPI = EV / AC$. The cost performance index is the earned value divided by the actual costs.

  Let us apply this formula to the situation above: See the formula applied here:

  $CPI = EV - AC$
  $CPI = \$40K / \$50K$
  $CPI = 0.80$

  The result is .80 or eighty percent efficient. If the result is less than one and performance continues at this rate, you will eventually run out of budget. If the result is one, your project is on track to finish on budget. If the result is greater than one, the project should finish under budget.

- **To complete performance index (TCPI).** The TCPI calculates the cost performance required to complete the remaining work within the budget. Once you determine this measure, you should be able to ask: can we achieve the performance required using our existing resources?

   The to complete performance index formula is: TCPI = (BAC – EV) / (BAC – AC).

   The "to complete performance index" is the budget at completion minus the earned value divided by the budget at completion minus the actual costs. In other words, the TCPI is the remaining work divided by the remaining budget.

   Let us apply this formula to the situation above. See the formula applied here:

   TCPI = (BAC – EV) / (BAC – AC)
   TCPI = ($100K - $40K) / ($100K - $50K)
   TCPI = $60K / $50K
   TCPI = 1.20

   The result in this situation is 1.20 or 120 percent. This means that cost performance would have to be increased from 80 percent (the current CPI) to 120 percent without adding resources. Is this realistic? It depends. If it is early enough in the project, the project team may be able to adjust and improve performance. But if it is late in the project, it is probably unrealistic.

If the TCPI is greater than 1.0, this is not a favorable result. It indicates that the project is having cost performance issues and must take action to get back on track.

You can also use an alternate version of this formula to consider what-if scenarios.

The alternate version of the formula is:

TCPI = (BAC – EV) / (EAC – AC).

The TCPI is the budget at completion minus the earned value divided by the estimate at completion minus the actual costs. In this alternate version of the formula, you substitute the BAC with an EAC. The EAC is an estimate at completion.

Going back to our situation, if we propose an estimate of completion (or a new proposed budget) of $115,000 (as opposed to the original budget of $100,000), then the formula would be applied as shown here:

TCPI = (BAC – EV) / (EAC – AC)
TCPI = ($100K - $40K) / ($115K - $50K)
TCPI = $60K / $65K
TCPI = 0.92

The result is 0.92 or 92 percent. This means that the cost performance in this situation must be improved from 80 percent to 92 percent in order to achieve the $115,000 estimate at completion.

## Schedule Performance

For schedule performance, we will review two formulas: schedule variance (SV) and the schedule performance index (SPI).

- **Schedule variance (SV).** Using earned value, the schedule variance formula will provide an assessment of the work performed against the work that was planned. The schedule variance will indicate whether the project is ahead of schedule or behind schedule in completing the work of the project.

  The schedule variance formula is:

  $$SV = EV - PV.$$

  Schedule variance is equal to earned value minus the planned value. The planned value is the work that was planned to be performed by the status reporting date.

  Let us apply this formula to the situation above. We will assume, for the purpose of this example, that the planned value is $45,000.

  $$SV = EV - PV$$
  $$SV = \$40K - \$45K$$
  $$SV = \$(5K)$$

  The result is negative five thousand dollars. This indicates that the project is running behind schedule. A negative result is unfavorable and indicates the project is running behind schedule. A result of zero indicates the project is on schedule. A result greater that one indicates that the project is ahead of schedule.

- **Schedule performance index (SPI).** The schedule performance index measures schedule efficiency and is used to help determine if the project completion date will be achieved. Once you have determined the schedule efficiency or the SPI, then you should be able to ask: if we continue at this rate, will we complete the project in time or not?

The schedule performance index formula is:

SPI = EV / PV.

The schedule performance index is the earned value divided by the planned value.

Let us apply this formula to the situation above:

See the formula applied here:

SPI = EV / PV
SPI = $40K / $45K
SPI = 0.89

The result is .89 or 89 percent efficient. If the result is less than one, this is not favorable and if this performance continues, you will be late on the project. If the result is one, your project is on track to finish on time. If the result is greater than one, this is a favorable variance and if this performance continues, you will finish earlier than planned.

## Forecasting

For forecasting, we will review three formulas: Estimate at completion (EAC), Variance at completion (VAC), and Estimate to complete (ETC).

- **Estimate at Completion (EAC).** The estimate at completion formula calculates the forecasted costs for the project. We will review four alternative methods of determining the EAC:

    o **EAC = AC + Bottom-up ETC.** The estimate to complete is equal to the actual costs plus the bottom-up estimate for the remaining work of the project. This formula may be best in a situation where the original plan is no longer valid, and remaining work needs to be re-estimated.

    As an example, if the actual costs are $50,000 and the team re-estimates the remaining work at $65,000, then the EAC would be $115,000.

    o **EAC = AC + (BAC – EV).** The estimate to complete is equal to actual costs plus the budget at completion minus the earned value. This formula would be used if the remaining work will be accomplished at the same rate as originally planned. This formula assumes the project incurred a one-time variance. In this example, the cost variance is negative $10K and the calculated EAC is $110K, which is the original BAC plus the one-time variance of $10K.

EAC = AC + (BAC − EV)
EAC = $50K + ($100K - $40K)
EAC = $110K

- o **EAC = BAC / CPI**. The estimate to complete is equal to the budget at completion divided by the cost performance index. This formula is used when the cost performance rate is expected to continue for the remainder of the project.

  For example, if the BAC is $100K and the CPI is 80 percent, then the EAC would be $125K.

- o **EAC = AC + [(BAC − EV) / (CPI * SPI)].** The estimate to complete is actual costs plus the amount calculated by dividing the budget at completion minus earned value by the product of the cost performance index and the schedule performance index. This formula may be used when both the cost performance and the schedule performance influence the estimate at completion.
- **Variance at completion (VAC).** This formula compares the forecasted costs against the original budget.

The variance at completion formula is:

VAC = BAC – EAC.

Variance at completion is the budget at completion minus the estimate at completion. A positive result indicates the budget will come in under budget. A zero variance determines the project will come in at the budgeted amount. A negative variance indicates that the project will come in over budget.

- **Estimate to complete (ETC).** This formula determines the expected cost to complete the work of the project.

  If a bottom-up estimate to complete is not used, then the formula for ETC is:

  ETC = EAC – AC.

  The estimate to complete is the estimate at completion minus the actual costs.

  For example, if the estimate at completion is $125K and the actual costs are $50K, then the ETC is $75K. In other words, $75K is required to complete the work of the project.

**Takeaways and a Prompt List**

The key takeaways from this chapter include the following:

- The three formulas for cost variance are the cost variance (CV) formula, the cost performance index (CPI) formula, and the "to complete performance index" (TCPI) formula.
- The two formulas for schedule performance are the schedule variance (SV) formula, and the schedule performance index (SPI) formula.
- The three formulas for forecasting are the estimate at completion (EAC), variance at completion (VAC), and the estimate to complete (ETC) formulas.

Consider the following prompt list of questions as you consider the implementation of EVM for your project or organization:

- Do your projects and your organizations apply the formulas presented in this chapter?
- Determining an EAC formula requires choosing a preferred formula based on the situation. Are your project managers sufficiently trained and experienced to choose the appropriate method?

# Chapter 10

# EVM Reports

Project status reporting can be subjective. Status reports may indicate optimistic outcomes without having the appropriate supporting evidence.

For example, the project manager for a project with a $125,000 budget may report that the project is within budget because actual costs incurred for the project to date are $50,000. The problem with that status is that it does not take earned value into account. Without knowing the project earned value, the status only indicates that $50,000 of the $125,000 budget has been spent. Earned value management provides an objective status of the cost performance. If the earned value in this example project is $40,000, then the objective report of the cost performance will indicate a negative cost variance of $10,000 (earned value of $40,000 minus the actual costs of $50,000). This variance tells us that the project spent $50,000 but only completed $40,000 of work.

Earned value management provides variances and metrics which can be used to provide objective status reporting.

Earned value can be compared against actual costs to determine cost variance and cost performance. Earned value can also be compared against the planned value to determine schedule variance and schedule performance.

Effective earned value reporting will provide the following:

- The original project budget (called the Budget at Completion).
- The original budget for each control account. The sum of the control accounts will equal the total project budget.
- The actual costs incurred as of the status reporting date. This should be reported by control account and by total project.
- The planned value for each control account and the overall project as of the reporting date.
- The cost variance for each control account and the overall project.
- The cost performance index for each control account and the overall project.
- The schedule variance for each control account and the overall project.
- The schedule performance index for each control account and the overall project.
- The TCPI for each control account and the overall project.
- The estimate at completion (EAC) for each control account and the overall project.
- The variance at completion for each control account and the overall project.

## EVM Report

We will take a look at a sample EVM report. An EVM report can provide a clear understanding of schedule and cost variances. Variances that exceed the tolerance limits are highlighted and provide the basis for making decisions and taking action.

Although an EVM report can be organized any number of ways, the best practice is to organize the reporting around the control accounts. This provides a clearer understanding of the control accounts that require attention. See exhibit 10,1 for an example of an EVM report summarizing performance by control account.

Project Enterprise: Week 12 of 20

| C.A. | BAC | PV | EV | AC | CPI | SPI |
|------|------|------|------|------|------|------|
| CA-1 | $40K | $25K | $25K | $25K | 1.00 | 1.00 |
| CA-2 | $25K | $18K | $15K | $20K | 0.75 | 0.83 |
| CA-3 | $50K | $30K | $30K | $30K | 1.00 | 1.00 |
| CA-4 | $80K | $50K | $50K | $51K | 0.98 | 1.00 |
| Sum | $195K | $123K | $120K | $126K | 0.95 | 0.98 |

**Tolerance level for CPI & SPI is .95 to 1.05**

Exhibit 10.1: EVM Report

As you can see from the example in 10.1, the earned value formulas are applied for each control account and a summary level for the project is also provided. Notice that a tolerance level is stated in the report and any control account with performance outside the tolerance level will be highlighted. In this example, the control account called CA02 shows an unfavorable CPI and SPI. The other control accounts are within the acceptable tolerances.

**EVM Graph**

Graphs can also be used to visually represent the current state of the project using earned value metrics. See exhibit 10.2 for an example of an earned value graph.

Earning Earned Value

As you can see in this example earned value graph, this project is forecasted to be over budget and late on the schedule. This type of graph is useful for quickly and transparently sharing an objective status of the project. This graph can be complemented with a tabular EVM report.

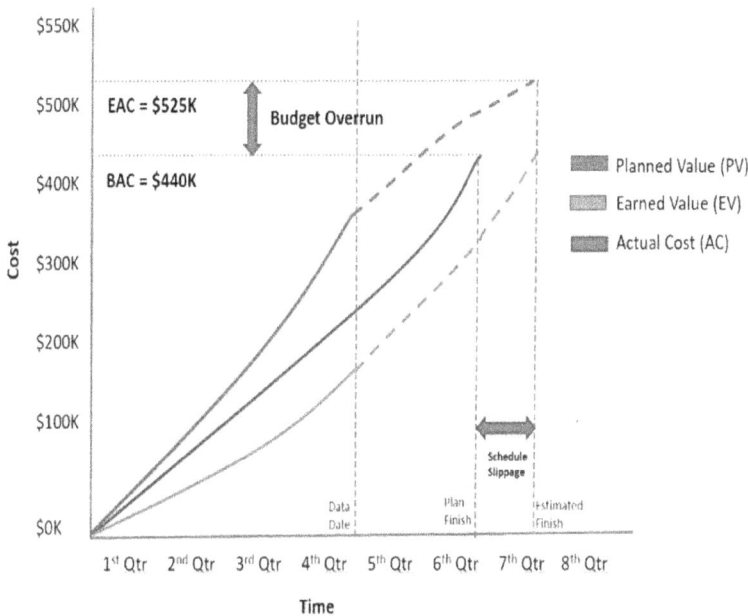

Exhibit 10.2: EVM Graph

**Unacceptable Variance**

Earned value reporting will highlight unacceptable variances from the performance measurement baseline. What corrections and updates are required to resolve these variances?

We will look at the following situations and review potential corrections and updates:

- Unacceptable negative cost performance variance
- Unacceptable positive cost performance variance
- Unacceptable negative schedule performance variance
- Unacceptable positive schedule performance variance

**Unacceptable negative cost performance variance.** If the cost performance index is less than 1.0 and exceeds the tolerance level for cost performance, consider the following actions, corrections, and updates:

- Determine which control accounts are causing the variance.
- Determine the root cause of the variance. Potential root causes can include but are not limited to: using more resources than planned, unexpected additional expenses, unplanned scope expansion, unplanned overtime, insufficient contingency reserve, unexpected risks, and poor estimates.
- Determine the estimate at completion (EAC) due to the variance.
- Review the TCPI to determine if cost performance can be improved to bring the costs back to the original budget.
- If it is not realistic to bring the costs back to the original budget, consider updating the performance measurement baseline to increase the budget or to adjust the budget among control accounts. This may require submitting a change request along with the justification for the change.

**Unacceptable positive cost performance variance.** If the cost performance index is greater than 1.0 and exceeds the tolerance level for positive variance, consider the following actions, corrections and updates:

- Determine which control accounts are causing the variance.
- Determine the root cause of the variance. Potential root causes for a positive variance include but are not limited to: using less resources than planned, planned expenses were not used, scope was reduced, unexpected positive risks, and poor estimates.
- Determine the estimate at completion (EAC) due to the variance.
- Determine if the performance measurement baseline needs to be updated. This may require a change request along with the justification for the change.

**Unacceptable negative schedule performance variance.** If the schedule performance index is less than 1.0 and exceeds the tolerance level for schedule performance, consider the following actions, corrections, and updates:

- Determine which control accounts are causing the variance.
- Determine the root cause of the variance. Potential root causes can include but are not limited to: work taking more time than planned, unplanned scope expansion, schedule delays due to external influences, longer wait times for review or approval of work, insufficient schedule reserve, unexpected risks, and poor estimates.

- Consider adding resources to achieve the original schedule target. Adding resources may require moving resources from other control accounts or increasing costs by adding resources not already in the plan. In most cases, these actions will require a change request.
- Determine if the performance measurement baseline needs to be updated. This may require a change request along with the justification for the change.

**Unacceptable positive schedule performance variance.** If the schedule performance index is greater than 1.0 and exceeds the acceptable tolerance level, consider the following actions, corrections, and updates:

- Determine which control accounts are causing the variance.
- Determine the root cause of the variance. Potential root causes for a positive schedule variance include but are not limited to: work taking less time than planned, scope was reduced, unexpected positive risks, and poor estimates.
- Determine the estimate at completion (EAC) due to the variance.
- Determine if the performance measurement baseline needs to be updated. This may require a change request along with the justification for the change.

Additionally, for these situations, be sure to update lessons learned. The lessons learned will contribute to improving the estimating, risk, and earned value management processes.

**Takeaways and a Prompt List**

The key takeaways from this chapter include the following:

- EVM reporting can provide an objective summary of performance results.
- EVM tabular reports can summarize results by control account.
- An EVM graph can provide a visual summary of project performance. These visual summaries appeal to managers and executives.

Consider the following prompt list of questions as you consider the implementation of EVM for your project or organization:

- Do your projects and organizations support EVM reporting?
- Has your organization or PMO selected project management tools that can provide EVM reports and graphs?

# Chapter 11

# EVM for Agile Projects

Can we use EVM for Agile projects? Does the structure of EVM conflict with the principles of simplicity and flexibility of Agile. Yes, and yes. Using EVM for an agile project can be a project or organizational decision. An organization may want to use EVM to provide control and structure on an agile project requiring a significant investment of resources.

In this chapter, we will look at EVM for Agile projects and introduce EVM techniques which can be applied to Agile projects.

**Agile and EVM: A High-Level Overview**

The agile approach is a project management approach that is used to iteratively and incrementally develop products.

Some of the key characteristics of agile methodologies include the following:

- Embraces change for competitive advantage.
- Promotes frequent delivery of value and products.
- Favors shorter cycles of work (iterations or sprints).
- Promotes iterative and incremental development of products.
- Promotes transparency.
- Promotes daily interactions with customers.
- Promotes frequent and early feedback from customers.

- Favors an adaptive, exploratory approach.

The advantages of an agile methodology include:

- Responsive to customer feedback.
- Embraces change for competitive advantage.
- Shorter iterations allow for faster delivery of value.
- Shorter iterations allow for quicker customer feedback.
- Reduces risk early.
- Promotes collaborative work.
- Promotes continuous improvement.
- Promotes transparent communications.

*Disadvantages of Using Agile*

The disadvantages of an agile methodology include:

- Limited documentation.
- Demands more dedicated time from the team.
- Customers may not be willing to commit the time required to support the project.
- More difficult to measure progress.
- Not suited for projects that are complex and high risk.
- Not suited for projects with predefined outcomes.

When considering Earned Value Management (EVM) for Agile projects, let's consider some advantages and some limitations.

On the positive side, EVM brings a structured and objective framework to performance measurement, which can be particularly valuable in Agile's often fast-paced and adaptive environment.

By quantifying progress in terms of scope, schedule, and cost, EVM enables teams to provide transparent objective updates to stakeholders and leadership. This enhances visibility and supports more accurate forecasting as well as proactive risk management.

The integration of EVM can also help bridge the gap between traditional project controls and the iterative nature of Agile, providing leadership with reliable insights for decision-making.

However, there are challenges to adopting EVM in Agile settings. Agile projects typically prioritize working software and customer collaboration over extensive documentation and rigid controls, while EVM relies on the definition and measurement of detailed baselines. This can make it difficult to apply EVM metrics accurately, especially when requirements and deliverables evolve frequently.

Additionally, aligning Agile's flexible approach with EVM's structured reporting requires additional effort and adaptation from the team, potentially introducing complexity that conflicts with Agile's core principles of simplicity and responsiveness.

There is also a risk of focusing too heavily on quantitative measures overlooking the qualitative value Agile teams aim to deliver.

The benefits of integrating EVM for Agile projects include:

- Establishing clear definitions of scope, value, and deliverables per iteration or sprint.
- Aligning the Work Breakdown Structure (WBS), if used, with Agile artifacts (e.g., user stories, features).

- Using standardized measurements for completed work (e.g., story points or completed stories).
- Incorporating EVM metrics (PV, EV, AC) into sprint reviews and retrospectives.
- Aligning EVM metrics with Agile release planning.
- Leveraging Agile project management tools that support EVM reporting and visualization.
- Helps ensure buy-in and understanding among all project stakeholders.

## EVM for Agile Sprints or Releases?

While EVM can provide value at both the sprint and release levels, it is generally more practical for Agile releases than for individual sprints. This is because releases encompass a broader time horizon, allowing for a more holistic assessment of project progress and value realization.

Sprints, being short and focused increments, may not provide enough data points or variability in scope to make EVM metrics meaningful. The impact of a single user story's delay or a scope change is much larger in a sprint, potentially distorting EVM indicators and making trends difficult to analyze.

Additionally, if the sprints are timeboxed (as in Scrum), the costs and schedule are fixed. Even if the EVM indicated a schedule delay, time-boxed sprints do not get extended. Alternatively, Agile teams typically use burndown charts (see Exhibit 11.1). Burndown charts track the remaining work and forecast whether the team is on track to complete the work within the timebox.

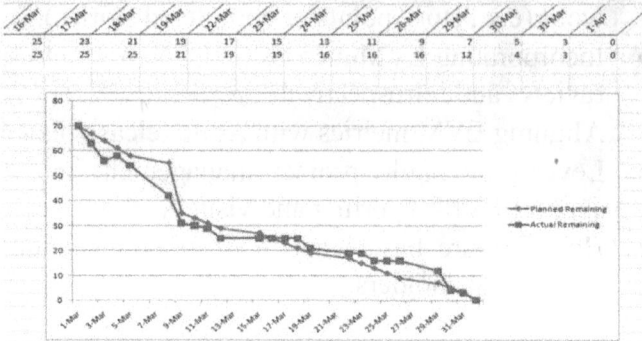

Exhibit 11.1: Example Burndown Chart

At the release level, however, the cumulative nature of EVM aligns well with Agile's iterative delivery model. Progress, cost, and value can be tracked over several sprints, smoothing out anomalies and enabling more accurate forecasting, performance measurement, and stakeholder reporting. The aggregation of work over multiple sprints allows earned value metrics to better reflect actual progress towards business objectives and leads to improved decision making for the release objectives.

## Determining Planned Value (PV)

In Agile projects, Planned Value (PV) represents the authorized budget assigned to scheduled work up to a specific point in time. To determine PV, Agile teams typically map the release plan or product backlog against the project timeline, assigning a budget or value to each user story, feature, or iteration. This can be done using story points, team-defined value units, or direct monetary assignments to backlog items.

For example, if a release consists of 1,000 story points and the project spans five sprints, the PV at the end of sprint two would be the total budgeted value for the stories scheduled (and planned to be completed) by that point, regardless of actual progress. If the total project budget is $50K and if the stories are balanced over the five sprints, then by the end of sprint two, the planned value would be $20K ($10K x 2).

## Determining Earned Value (EV)

When determining earned value (EV) on Agile projects, traditional methods such as percent-complete or work package valuation can be adapted to fit the iterative, incremental nature of Agile.

Let's take a look at three practical approaches used to calculate EV in Agile environments:

- Story Points-Based Earned Value: This method leverages the story points assigned to user stories or backlog items. At the close of each iteration (sprint), the EV is calculated as the sum of story points for all completed stories. For example, if a sprint delivers 20 story points out of a 100-point release plan, the EV is 20% of the total planned value.

  Alternatively, a story point value can be determined based on the budget divided by the number of planned story points. For example, if the budget is $50K and the number of story points planned is 200, then the value of each story point is $250. Earned value can be calculated by multiplying the number of story points completed times $250. If 20 story points have been completed, then the EV is $5K.

- Monetized Value Delivery: Agile teams may assign a monetary value to each feature or story, reflecting business value or customer impact. The EV at any point is the sum of the monetary values of all completed features or stories.

- Milestone or Feature-Based Earned Value: For larger Agile initiatives, EV can be tracked by the completion of significant features or milestones, with each milestone representing a portion of the total planned value.

Each method must be tailored to the project's context, team maturity, and stakeholder needs. It is critical that only completed stories, features, or increments are counted toward earned value. Partially finished work does not contribute to EV in Agile.

**Determining Actual Costs (AC)**

In Agile projects, determining Actual Costs (AC) involves capturing all expenses incurred to complete the work up to a specific point in time. This includes salaries or contractor fees for team members, costs for software licenses, infrastructure, and any other resources directly associated with the project's delivery during each iteration or sprint. Typically, teams aggregate the costs on a sprint-by-sprint basis, aligning expenditures with the work actually performed. The most common approach is to track labor costs, as these usually represent the bulk of Agile project expenses. For example, if a sprint team consists of six members working two weeks, the AC would be the sum of each member's cost for that sprint duration, plus any additional project-related expenses incurred during the same period.

Accurate and timely recording of these costs enables effective comparison with planned and earned values, allowing project managers to monitor variances and manage budgets proactively.

**Agile Cost Formulas**

The formula for **cost variance (CV)** on an agile project is:

$CV = EV - AC$

Where EV is the (% story points completed X Budget)

OR the story point value X the story points completed.

Example:

- Total Budget = $100K.
- 50% of the story points have been completed.
- Actual costs = $55K

The Cost Variance (CV) is:

$CV = (50\% \times \$100K) - \$55K$

$CV = -\$5K$ (negative $5K)

The project is over budget.

The formula for **cost performance (CPI)** on an agile project is:

$CPI = EV / AC$

Continuing the example, the CPI would be calculated as:

CPI = (50% X $100K) / $55K

CPI = .91

The cost performance is unfavorable. If this performance continues, the team will run out of budget before the work is completed.

**Agile Schedule Formulas**

The formula for **schedule variance (SV)** on an agile project is:

SV = EV – PV

OR: SV = (value of story points completed / value of story points planned)

Where EV is the (% story points completed X Budget)

OR the story point value X the story points completed.

Example:

- Total budget is $100K
- Planned Value = $60K (60% X $100K)
- EV = 50% X $100K

The Schedule Variance (SV) is:

SV = EV – PV

SV = $50K - $60K

SV = - $10K (negative $10K)

The project is running behind schedule.

The formula for **schedule performance (SPI)** on an agile project is:

SPI = EV / PV

Continuing the example, the SPI would be calculated as:

SPI = (50% X $100K) / $60K

SPI = .83

The schedule performance is unfavorable. If this performance continues, the team will need more time (additional unplanned sprints) to complete the work.

**Situational Case Example**

Let's try a situational case example. Part 1 will provide the situation, the data, and will provide the EVM questions. Part 2 will provide the answers.

*Part 1 – The Situation*

An agile project to develop a new product for a financial organization has planned to complete 1200 story points over 20 weeks. The team has calculated that each story point has a value of $50. Each iteration is time-boxed for one week.

After the 10th week, 500 story points have been completed and the actual expenditure is $25,000.

Questions:

1. What is the BAC (budget at completion)?
2. What is the current earned value?
3. What is current PV (planned value)?
4. What is the CPI (cost performance index)?

5. What is the SPI (schedule performance index)?
6. What is the project status (budget and schedule)?

*Part 2 – The Answers*

1. What is the BAC (budget at completion)? Answer:
   total story points X story point value
   $BAC = 1200 \times \$50$
   $BAC = \$60K$.

2. What is the current earned value? Answer:
   # story points completed X story point value
   $EV = 500 \times \$50$
   $EV = \$25K$

3. What is current PV (planned value)? Answer:
   $PV$ = sprint value x 10 sprints completed
   $PV = \$3K \times 10$
   $PV = \$30K$

4. What is the CPI (cost performance index)? Answer:
   $CPI = EV / AC$
   $CPI = \$25K / \$25K$
   $CPI = 1.0$
   The project is on budget.

5. What is the SPI (schedule performance index)?
   Answer:
   $SPI = EV / PV$
   $SPI = \$25K / \$30K$
   $SPI = .83$

6. What is the project status (budget and schedule)?
   Answer: The project is on budget but behind schedule.

## Summary

This chapter explored how Earned Value Management (EVM) can be adapted for agile projects. It discusses the compatibility and challenges of merging EVM's structured approach with agile's flexible, iterative methods. Key points include the benefits of using EVM for objective tracking, forecasting, and stakeholder communication, as well as the potential difficulties due to Agile's evolving requirements and emphasis on working software.

The chapter covers practical techniques for calculating EVM metrics such as Planned Value (PV), Earned Value (EV), and Actual Cost (AC) using story points, features, or monetary values assigned to agile deliverables. It explains how these metrics can be applied at sprint or release levels, and provides formulas for assessing cost and schedule performance.

A situational example illustrates applying EVM to a real agile project, showing how to calculate budget at completion, earned value, planned value, and performance indices. Ultimately, the chapter highlights both the opportunities and challenges of integrating EVM into agile, emphasizing the need to tailor the appropriate approach for each project.

**Takeaways and a Prompt List**

The key takeaways from this chapter include the following:

- EVM can be used to track progress on an Agile project.
- EVM metrics such as Planned Value (PV), Earned Value (EV), and Actual Cost (AC) can be determined using story points, features, or monetary values assigned to agile deliverables.
- EVM can be used more effectively at the release or project level than at the sprint level.

Consider the following prompt list of questions as you consider the implementation of EVM for your project or organization:

- If your organization uses agile methods for projects, can EVM add value for determining progress?
- How would you convince your agile teams and leadership on the value of EVM for agile projects?

# Chapter 12

# Implementing EVM

In this chapter, we will explore a high-level step-by-step approach to implementing an earned value management system. We will first address implementing an EVM system for a single project in an organization with a lack of formal project management experience and no Project Management Office (PMO). We will then explore implementing EVM for an organization with a low project management maturity level.

Let's start with implementing EVM for a single project.

## Implementing EVM for a Single Project

Let us assume for the purpose of this section that you will be managing a project in an organization with a lack of formal project management experience and no Project Management Office (PMO).

The project is a critical project that requires a major investment of organizational resources and costs. The project is an ideal candidate for an EVM system to control costs and time on the project.

How would you implement an EVM system for this project?

Let's look at a step-by-step approach.

*Step 1: Understand the Organizational Context*

- Review the Project Charter, if one has been developed to understand the project goals, objectives, challenges, and key stakeholders.
- Meet with the project sponsor and other key leaders and managers to confirm the project's vision and objectives.
- Assess available resources, tools, and staff capabilities.
- Assess the organization's readiness for change to a structured project management approach and EVM. Identify potential champions within the organization.

*Step 2: Educate and Engage Key Stakeholders*

- Conduct awareness sessions on the benefits and fundamentals of EVM for both leadership and project teams.
- Educate the team members on the key concepts and formulas for EVM.
- Train team members on the practices, such as disciplined detailed planning and regular updates required (such as hours worked, percent completions, deliverables completed, and costs incurred).
- Educate any partners, suppliers, and vendors of the EVM requirements. The EVM requirements may affect the terms of the contracts (such as percent complete, and hours worked).
- Establish buy-in for EVM as a tool for improved performance reporting and control, better decision-making, transparency, and accountability.

*Step 3: Clearly Define the Project Scope, Schedule, and Budget*

- Work with stakeholders to clearly document the project scope, deliverables, scope exclusions, and acceptance criteria. Create a formal project scope statement for approval.
- Using the approved project scope statement as a guide, decompose the work of the project into manageable components or work packages. Create a work breakdown structure (WBS) which defines control accounts and work packages in a hierarchical organization. Develop the WBS dictionary which provides the detail to support the WBS. Review the WBS with the team and stakeholders. Seek approval for the Scope Baseline, which consists of the Project Scope Statement, the WBS, and the WBS dictionary.
- Using the Scope Baseline as a foundation, create a detail schedule of project activities required to complete the work of the project. The schedule should include project milestones and should clearly identify activity dependencies so that a schedule critical path can be determined. Seek approval of the schedule to create the Schedule Baseline.
- Develop a realistic cost estimates of the work to performed on the project. Aggregate the estimates, allocate budgets to the work to be performed, and determine a time-phased budget or Cost Baseline. Seek approval of the Cost Baseline.

*Step 4: Build the Performance Measurement Baseline*

- Integrate the scope, schedule, and budget into a single baseline document (the PMB).
- Assign measurable values (such as story points, hours, or dollars) to each work package or deliverable.
- Ensure all planned work is mapped to the baseline and that it is approved by key stakeholders.
- Document the baseline in accessible tools or spreadsheets if formal EVM software is not available.
- Present the PMB to the team and key decision makers.

*Step 5: Establish Data Collection and Reporting Processes*

- Define how progress will be measured (e.g., percent complete, deliverable acceptance, or agile story points completed).
- Set up simple procedures for collecting Actual Cost, tracking Planned Value, and calculating Earned Value.
- Determine a reporting cadence (e.g., weekly, bi-weekly, or monthly status meetings).
- Train the team on how to capture and report progress consistently.
- Set up controls and procedures to ensure compliance with data collection and reporting processes.

*Step 6: Monitor Project Progress*

- Compare actual performance against the baseline at regular intervals.
- Calculate EVM metrics:

- o Schedule Variance (SV): $EV - PV$
- o Cost Variance (CV): $EV - AC$
- o Schedule Performance Index (SPI): $EV / PV$
- o Cost Performance Index (CPI): $EV / AC$
- o To-complete-performance Index (TCPI): $(BAC - EV) / (BAC - AC)$.

- Visualize progress using simple charts or dashboards, even if only in spreadsheets.
- Review findings with the team and management, highlighting variances, trends, and risks.

*Step 7: Control and Update Baselines*

- Define a formal process for change control: document, review, and approve any changes to scope, schedule, or budget before updating the baseline.
- Re-baseline only when significant, unavoidable changes occur, ensuring all stakeholders approve the update.
- Communicate changes and their impact on performance to the team and leadership.

*Step 8: Support Continuous Improvement*

- At project milestones or closure, review EVM practices and document lessons learned.
- Solicit feedback from the team and stakeholders to refine processes for future projects.
- Share successes and improvements with leadership to encourage a culture of project management maturity.

*Summary*

In summary, by following these steps, a project manager can establish reliable project controls even in a low maturity organization. The project manager can then contribute to organizational growth by sharing successes and challenges in the implementation of a an EVM system for a major project.

## Implementing EVM for an Organization

Let us assume for the purpose of this section that you will be implementing EVM for an organization with a lack of formal project management experience and no Project Management Office (PMO).

Let us assume that the organization can benefit from an EVM system because the projects undertaken can be significant in costs and impacts.

How would you implement an EVM system for this organization?

Let's look at a step-by-step approach.

*Step 1: Gain Leadership Buy-In:*

- Begin by educating organizational leaders on the value and purpose of Earned Value Management (EVM).
- Quantify and share the benefits of EVM.
- Prepare concise presentations or workshops that highlight how EVM aligns with organizational goals and how it can contribute to the improvement of project performance and successful outcomes.

*Step 2: Establish a Core Implementation Team:*

> Identify a small group of motivated individuals, such as project managers, finance/accounting staff, and technical leads, who can and will champion the EVM initiative. Assign clear roles and responsibilities even in the absence of a formal PMO.

*Step 3: Develop Simple, Scalable EVM Guidelines:*

- Draft basic EVM procedures tailored to the organization's needs.
- Focus on the core concepts of planning: defining project scope, establishing a work breakdown structure (WBS), setting baseline schedules and budgets, and standardizing progress measurement methods.

*Step 4: Start with a Pilot Project:*

- Select a project with moderate complexity as a pilot.
- Apply EVM practices to this project, keeping documentation and metrics straightforward and accessible.
- Use this opportunity to refine templates, procedures, and reporting tools.
- Hold retrospectives throughout the project to reflect on successes and challenges.

*Step 5: Train the Project Team:*

- Provide hands-on training sessions on planning practices and EVM.

- Provide reference materials for all team members involved in the pilot.
- Emphasize the basics of tracking progress, updating cost and schedule data, and interpreting EVM metrics.

*Step 6: Monitor, Report, and Review:*

- Throughout the pilot, collect data on planned value (PV), earned value (EV), and actual cost (AC).
- Report EVM metrics regularly to all stakeholders.
- Hold brief review meetings to discuss findings, identify gaps, and adjust processes.

*Step 7: Document Lessons Learned from the Pilot:*

- At project completion, conduct a retrospective to capture successes, challenges, and improvement suggestions.
- Update the EVM guidelines based on feedback from the pilot team.

*Step 8: Incremental Rollout:*

- Gradually introduce EVM practices to additional projects, using lessons learned from the pilot to aid in adoption.
- Encourage knowledge sharing and peer mentoring among project teams.
- Prepare and share a presentation and/or workshop to review the pilot experience.

*Step 9. Build Toward Organizational Standards:*

- As experience grows, formalize EVM policies and procedures into a set of organizational standards.
- Consider establishing a lightweight governance function or virtual PMO focused on project controls and continuous improvement.

*Step 10. Foster Continuous Improvement:*

- Promote open communication about project performance, leveraging EVM results to drive decision-making and accountability.
- Celebrate milestones and visible improvements to reinforce the value of disciplined project management.
- In the absence of a PMO, consider establishing a champion for EVM standards.

*Summary*

In summary, by following the steps outlined here, it is possible to implement EVM for an organization with a lack of formal project management experience and no Project Management Office (PMO). This approach can lead to enhanced project predictability and long-term maturity.

**Takeaways and a Prompt List**

The key takeaways from this chapter include the following:

- EVM can be implemented for a single project in an organization with a lack of formal project management experience and no Project Management Office (PMO). All it requires is for the project manager to intentionally implement an EVM for improved project controls.

- EVM can be implemented at an enterprise level for an organization with a lack of formal project management experience and no Project Management Office (PMO). It does require an organization commitment to EVM and to a pilot project. Without a PMO, it will also require commitment from a champion or champions.

Consider the following prompt list of questions as you consider the implementation of EVM for your project or organization:

- Should your organization consider a cost/benefit analysis for implementing EVM for either a single project or at an enterprise level?
- In the absence of a PMO, can your organization identify individuals who can serve as champions for an EVM implementation?
- Should your organization consider a pilot project for EVM?

# Final Thoughts

Implementing and using EVM does not have to be confusing or complicated. With the aid of a few processes and a little bit of discipline, project managers can lead all of their projects to successful performance by incorporating the knowledge shared in this book.

My hope is that you will begin using the concepts presented in this book to enhance your planning practices and to improve the performance of your projects.

Additionally, I hope that you will continue to use this book as a guide for your EVM efforts as well as an educational tool for your project teams.

I wish you success with your projects and your personal development journeys!

Thanks,

Eddie Merla, PMP

Author of: "Get Project Smart! A Leader's Guide to Unlocking the Secrets of Project management."

Co-Author of: "Communicate, Lead, and Transform: Behaviors to Break Free from Your Mental Wheel Ruts."

# Index

# Project Training and Services

We offer the following project management training programs:

- Building High Performance Teams (1/2 Day)
- Conflict Management for Project Managers (1/2 Day)
- Effective Meeting Management (1/2 Day)
- Earning Earned Value Workshop (One day)
- Introduction to Agile/Scrum (One Day)
- Introduction to Project Management (One Day)
- Project Management for Leaders (One Day)
- Project Risk Management Workshop (One Day)
- Power Skills for Business and Technical Professionals (Two Days)
- Agile Project Management (Three Days)
- Fundamentals of Project Management (Three Days)
- Project Management Professional (PMP®) Preparation (Four Days)

Besides project management training, we provide PMO startup support, short-term PMO augmentation, virtual PMO support for small to medium-sized organizations, project management coaching, and transition support from traditional project management to Agile methods.

For more information on our training or services, contact us at: training@duendepm.com